For
Christians
Who Are
Seriously Dating

OR WOULD LIKE TO BE

For
Christians
Who Are
Seriously Dating

OR WOULD LIKE TO BE

◆

Questions Every Christian Should Ask Before Getting Engaged To Be Married

◆

Elreta Dodds

Press Toward The Mark Publications
Detroit Michigan

For Christians who are Seriously Dating or Would Like to Be

ISBN: 0-9660390-3-3
Library of Congress Control Number: 2003097287

Editors
Noreta Dennard
Dr. Stephanie Stevenson

Cover Design
Leisia Duskin, Detroit Michigan

Acknowledgements...

A very Special Thanks to my editors, Noreta Dennard and Dr. Stephanie Stevenson. Your voluntary willingness to tackle the tedious and time-consuming task of making sure the grammar, spelling, and organization of the text are correct is priceless.

For their critiques, Specials Thanks, in alphabetical order, to Noreta Dennard, Yvonne Janet Gillom, Derek Maurice Grigsby, Pastor Emery Moss Jr., Dr. Stephanie Stevenson, and Minister Jeffrey Alan Williams. Your time, energy, and effort are greatly appreciated. I can't thank you enough for your support and encouragement.

Again, Special Thanks to my beloved sister, Noreta Dennard, for helping me brainstorm the title, for your artistic eye, and for helping me sort through cover graphics, fonts, and color. Your input has been paramount in leading me towards, what I think, is a great looking cover.

Special Thanks to Leisia Duskin for your cover design, for putting up with all of my idiosyncrasies, and for being willing to stay up late on more than a couple of occasions with my sister and I as the three of us muddled over cover samples while drinking coffee and eating Chinese food.

Special Thanks to Jean Schroeder and Kathy King of Sheridan Books for all of your expertise, assistance, and patience throughout the years.

Special Thanks to Barb Gunia of Sans Serif Incorporated for working with me on this one too and for all of your expertise, assistance, and patience over the years as well.

OTHER BOOKS IN PRINT WRITTEN BY ELRETA DODDS

Is God a Chauvinist?
The Bible and Women: A Complete Look
(May 2002, ISBN: 0-9660390-2-5)

- Aimed at dispelling the notion that the Bible is a chauvinistic and sexist book, as well as at challenging the belief that the Bible adds to the oppression that women experience to some degree in almost every society of the world.

What the Bible really says about Slavery:
This and other information on the issue of Slavery as it applies to History and Religion
(January 2000, ISBN: 0-9660390-1-7)

- Argues against the belief of some that say the Bible teaches that blacks are cursed to be slaves and that Christianity "the white man's religion." The book takes the reader from Christian apologetics to historical slavery through a comprehensive analysis of scripture, and even through the Civil War.

The Trouble with Farrakhan and the Nation of Islam:
Another Message to the Black Man in America
(November 1997, ISBN: 0-9660390-0-9)

- Contends that Louis Farrakhan's 1995 Million Man March was little more than a tool used to propagate Nation of Islam theology under the guise of a push towards improved black solidarity. Argues against the Nation of Islam's accusation that Christianity is nothing but a "black slave-making religion." Categorizes Farrakhan and his "Nation" as racist and anti-Christian and biblically discusses excerpts from four of Farrakhan's landmark speeches (including his address at the March) to prove it.

TABLE OF CONTENTS

Introduction......................... i.

1.
Preliminary Questions.............. p.1

2.
Religion.............................. p.7

3.
Lifestyle............................. p.21

4.
The "Ex" Factor.................... p.51

5.
Family and Friends................. p.60

6.
Children............................. p.70

7.
Work, Finances, and Money...... p.81

8.
Division of Labor
in and Outside of the Home...   P.101

9.
Sex and Sex Appeal..................   p.106

10.
Domestic Violence..................   p.130

11.
What if?.............................   p.150

12.
Personality p.154

13.
Other Important Questions.........   p.167

14.
Write your own Chapter.................... p.180

INTRODUCTION

You are now holding your very own compatibility journal. This book is designed to measure how compatible you are with the person you are dating. It is a book of questions specifically designed for Christian men and women who are in a dating relationship, are serious about the person they are dating, and are therefore thinking about getting engaged to be married. The book is also intended for single Christians who are not dating but would like to eventually begin a serious relationship with someone one day. The questions in this book will help them to keep in mind certain things that they may want to consider should they ever establish a relationship that they feel might be headed towards the altar. Those who are already engaged will also find this book helpful. And although this book is geared towards Christians, non-Christians will be able to benefit from it too.

The questions in this book are open-ended and they ask very specific things about you and about the person you are dating. After each question, a space is provided for you in order that you may write down answers. Some questions are given more space for an answer than other questions.

A little while back, I lectured at a Christian singles event in which I presented a list of questions that I feel Christians who are seriously dating should ask of the person they are dating. When the lecture was over, there were many attendees who asked me for a copy of my questions. So instead of giving them a loose paper copy, I decided to put the questions in the form of a book. This is that book.

To make the best of this book, the person you are dating (who will henceforth be referred to as your *significant other*) should also have his or her own copy of the book so that he or she can ask the same questions of you. This way, the two of you will be able to compare notes and both of you will have something tangible to reflect on when examining and considering whether or not the two of you really are compatible. It is essential that both you and your significant other answer these questions truthfully when presenting them to one another.

For our purposes, a couple is seriously dating if that couple has gone out together or has seen each other several times *and* has decided to date one another exclusively *for* the purposes of determining whether or not the two of them want to take it further. They are an item. They are seeing one another beyond a casual date here and there. They are courting one another. They're not engaged yet, but things are getting pretty serious.

For some time I have felt that premarital counseling for Christians is often times not extensive enough. Not only is it not extensive enough but it is also frequently offered to a couple when they are already engaged. And while there are many engagements that look very promising there are many other engagements that should be broken.

However, appealing to the expectation of others and saving face probably play significant roles in the hesitation to break off an engagement that should be broken, not to mention all of the money that has been spent already towards the engagement and the impending marriage. Furthermore, breaking an engagement is psychologically and socially very hard to do. It is very difficult to call off an engagement after you've announced to all your friends, family, coworkers, and whoever else, that you're getting married... after you've set a date, after you and your intended have bought rings, and so on.

This is why I believe that premarital counseling should take place during what I call the "seriously dating" stage *before* a couple becomes engaged. This way, a couple can more graciously investigate whether or not they are "meant for each other." This book is designed to help do that.

This does not mean that engaged couples cannot benefit from the book. As stated earlier, engaged couples can benefit from this book, as long as they answer the questions honestly, just as much as couples who are not yet engaged can. And although some people think that couples should not ask these questions of one another until they are engaged, there is no doubt (especially when taking into account the reasons previously cited) that it is wiser to ask as many questions as you can, and get as much information about your significant other as possible, before any engagement takes place.

There are nine basic areas of compatibility that are presented in this book. These include but are not limited to religion, lifestyle, division of labor in the home, family and friends, children, work/finances/money, sex, and personality. If you find that the two of you are grossly incompatible in any one of these major areas, without much promise for successful compromising, then you should think twice before taking your relationship any further. A chapter that provides questions for the purpose of revealing whether or not your significant other has a tendency towards domestic violence is also included. There is also space at the end of the book for you to create your own chapter. You will be able to write down questions (and the answers to those questions) that may be important to you that I may have missed.

You won't be able to get through this book in a day because the book will arouse a great deal of discussion between you and your significant other (which is what it's supposed to do). However, if you want to get through the book quickly, it's possible to go through it on a daily basis and complete it in a couple of weeks (one chapter per day). But, it's best to take your time and give yourself at least a couple of months, if not more than a couple of months. You're going to be asking each other some very important questions, and it will not benefit either of you to rush through. Ideally one to two weeks should be given to each area of compatibility (each chapter) in order that the two of you may talk over the answers to the questions thoroughly.

It should be emphasized though, that this book is not necessarily intended to take the place of a premarital counseling session with your pastor or with a Christian counselor. The book should be used as part of the counseling experience itself and to enhance it. It would be best for the two of you to go through this book together with a Christian counselor, minister, or pastor to help you along. However, if for some reason, you are unable or unwilling to involve the assistance of a counselor, this book can stand alone as a self-help to aid you (as long as both of you are honest when answering the questions) in making an informed decision as to whether or not to allow the relationship to progress further.

When it comes to asking and answering the questions that are presented in this book, it should be emphasized that the two of you will not agree or be compatible on every point. But if there is gross incompatibility in any of the major areas that are presented, then it might be time to rethink the relationship.

Before delving into questions of compatibility, some women prefer to wait until the man proposes marriage. And most men don't even want to utter the word *marriage* until they're ready to propose. If you feel uncomfortable asking your significant other these questions before getting engaged and you'd rather wait until the question is "popped" (whether you're the one who "pops" it or whether you're the one waiting for it to be "popped") then at least sit down and go through this book before *announcing* your engagement, before *telling anyone*, and before either of you begin *wearing an engagement ring*.

Don't forget that engagements are hard to break so you want to find out just how compatible the two of you are before you tell everyone that you're going to be married.

Well, it's time to begin asking yourself and your significant other about the stuff that you really need to know. Remember, be honest!

1.

SOME PRELIMINARY QUESTIONS

Before we get started in the specific areas of compatibility that are presented in this book, it is important that you ask your significant other the following preliminary questions. These questions don't necessarily fit under any particular area of compatibility, but they are important questions, all the same.

Why are you dating your significant other? Why is he or she dating you? How long have the two of you been dating? Has it been long enough?

_____
_____
_____
_____
_____
_____

Are you in love with your significant other? Is he or she in love with you? What does being "in love" mean to you? To your significant other?

_____
_____
_____
_____
_____
_____

Do you love your significant other as outlined in 1St Corinthians chapter 13? If so, in which ways? If not, why not?

_____

_____

_____

_____

_____

_____

Does your significant other love you as outlined in 1st Corinthians 13? If so, in what ways? If not, why not?

_____

_____

_____

_____

_____

_____

Have you told your significant other that you love him or her? If not, why not?

_____

_____

_____

Has your significant other told you that he or she loves you? If not, why not?

_____

_____

_____

Is marriage something that you have been asking God for? Is marriage something that your significant other has been asking God for? If so, why do you want to get married? If your significant other has also been asking God for marriage, why does he or she want to get married?

_____

_____

_____

_____

_____

_____

Do you enjoy your significant other's company? Does he or she enjoy your company?

_____

_____

_____

Do you genuinely like your significant other? If so, what is it about him or her that you like?

_____

_____

_____

_____

_____

Does he or she genuinely like you? If so, what is it about you that he or she likes?

_____

_____

_____

_____

_____

What is there about your significant other that you don't particularly like? Be honest.

_____

_____

_____

_____

_____

_____

What is there about you that your significant other doesn't particularly like?

_____

_____

_____

_____

_____

_____

Are you empathic and/or compassionate towards your significant other (can you easily put yourself in his or her place in order to understand what he or she might be going through)? If so, in what way? Does your significant other agree that you are empathic? If you're not, empathic and/or compassionate, why aren't you?

_____

_____

_____

Do you feel that your significant other is empathic and/or compassionate towards you? If so, in what way? If not, why isn't he or she?

_____

_____

_____

Does your significant other want to be with you as much as you want to be with him or her? If not, why not?

_____

_____

_____

Do you want to be with your significant other as much as he or she wants to be with you? If not, why not?

_____

_____

_____

Do you confide in your significant other? If not, why not? Does he or she confide in you? If not, why not?

_____

_____

_____

Do you trust your significant other? If not, why not? Does he or she trust you? If not, why not?

_____

_____

_____

How long have you and your significant other been dating and do both of you think it has been long enough to get engaged?

_____

_____

_____

Aside from having a dating relationship, do you look at your significant other as a friend? If so, in what way? If not, why not?

_____

_____

_____

_____

_____

Does he or she look at you as a friend? If so, in what way? If not, why not?

_____

_____

_____

_____

_____

If either one of you are disappointed with any of the answers of the other, then the two of you are not as compatible as you may have thought. There are certain things that a relationship should consist of that are important from the start.

Both you and your significant other should feel a certain amount of love for one another and it would be best if the intensity of your love for one another were similar. Also, the two of you should like each other, want to be together, be able to confide in one another, and consider the other one not just as a potential marriage partner, but as a friend as well. If these basic things are not present in the relationship, then it is best not to take the relationship any further. But if the two of you feel confident that these things are present, then you may progress to the next chapter.

2.

RELIGION

The Bible clearly tells us that we should not seek to establish close bonds with people who are not Christians. The reasons for this are rather obvious. God wants to make sure that we are not influenced by people who don't acknowledge him (The Father, Son, and Holy Ghost) as God. A devout Christian who is married to a devout Muslim will have many troubles in his or her marriage. The same applies to a Christian married to an atheist, an agnostic, a Jehovah's Witness, and so forth. The marriage will become even more complicated and problematic if and when children come along.

So, if you have found yourself seriously dating a person who is not a Christian, then it would be best to break off the relationship. This may seem harsh, but the Word of God is in favor of dissolving such a relationship as confirmed in 2nd Corinthians 6:14-15, which reads, *"Don't team up with those who are unbelievers. How can goodness be a partner with wickedness? How can light live with darkness? What harmony can there be between Christ and the Devil? How can a believer be a partner with an unbeliever?"* (NLT)

Paul didn't mince words here. He emphatically taught that Christians should not seek to bond with unbelievers and he likened unbelievers to wickedness, darkness, and the Devil. Certainly then, we as Christians, should not set our sights on marrying an unbeliever. And with this being the case, there would be no reason for us to date an unbeliever either.

However, some Christians believe that it is okay to date an unsaved person as long as they are witnessing to that unsaved person about the Lord. But the Word of God clearly indicates that this is not okay because as Christians, we are not even supposed to associate with *other Christians* who are living immoral lives.

1ˢᵗ Corinthians 5:9-11 attests to this and reads as follows: *"When I wrote you before, I told you not to associate with people who indulge in sexual sin. But I wasn't talking about unbelievers who indulge in sexual sin, or who are greedy, or are swindlers, or idol worshippers. You would have to leave this world to avoid people like that. What I meant was that you are not to associate with anyone who claims to be a Christian yet indulges in sexual sin, or is greedy, or worships idols, or is abusive, or a drunkard, or a swindler. Don't even eat with such people."* (NLT)

We cannot avoid associating with unbelievers because they are with us on our jobs, in our families, and so forth. An associate is different from a friend. A friend has a higher status than an associate does. There is a deeper bond. However, the above passage of scripture makes it clear that we, as Christians, should not *even associate* with those who call themselves Christians but live as though they are not. It follows, therefore, that we should also not seek to become close friends with those who are not Christians. Most of us would not be inclined to establish close friendships with people that our earthly father or mother identifies as enemies. Therefore it follows that we should also not be inclined to establish close friendships with people whom our spiritual Father identifies as enemies, and certainly therefore, not be inclined to marry them. With this said, it would be difficult to argue against the notion that we should not date anyone that is not saved.

Despite this, there are some Christians who are married to unbelievers for one reason for another. In these instances, the Bible teaches that the Christian should "stick it out" with his or her unbelieving spouse (as long as the unbeliever is willing to stay in the marriage) and set an example by living holy which will increase the probability that the unbelieving spouse will one day also confess Jesus as Lord/Savior and reap salvation (1ˢᵗ Corinthians 7:12-14).

8

It should be underscored that you're not necessarily out of the woods just because you're dating someone who is a Christian. If both of you are Christians but you disagree on many doctrines that are not necessarily essential to salvation, but all the same you still disagree, then such disagreements could cause a serious rift between the two of you if you were to marry one another. There is no doubt that the two of you would be arguing about the scriptures frequently, which wouldn't be a good thing. Aside from this, there are certain essential fundamental Christian doctrines that you and your significant other should agree on, without question, if both of you are calling yourselves Christians.

- *Essential doctrines of the Christian faith*

There are many people who call themselves Christians who are not really Christians. In order to be a true Christian, one must basically believe in the essential doctrines of the Christian faith. These essential doctrines are as follows:

- The Bible stands alone as the Word of God.
- The Bible is infallible.
- The Bible identifies who God is.
- God is identified in the Bible (Exodus 3:13-14) as "I AM THAT I AM" (Yahweh)
- There is no other God besides Yahweh (YHWH).
- There is one God who represents himself in and eternally exists in three beings/personages/persons (the Father, the Son, and the Holy Ghost)
- Jesus Christ is The Son (the second being/personage/person of the Godhead) who was manifest as a man thereby becoming God in the flesh during his first earthly coming (John 1:1-14)
- Jesus was born of the Virgin Mary.
- Jesus Christ is the Messiah prophesied of by the Old Testament prophets.

9

- Jesus came to redeem men and women from their sins by shedding his blood on the cross thus becoming the ultimate sin offering.
- Jesus rose bodily from the dead, three days after he died on the cross, thus proving his Deity.
- Jesus ascended into heaven after his resurrection to once again sit at the right hand side of the Father. (Mark 16:19)
- In order for one to be saved (go to heaven at physical death) one must confess that Jesus is Lord (God in the flesh) and believe in his or her heart that he rose from the dead. (Romans 10:9)
- Jesus is "the way, the truth, and the life," and the only way to the Father is through him. (John 14:6).

Do both of you agree with the essential doctrines of the Christian faith that are listed above? If you don't agree, which doctrines don't you agree with and why?

_____
_____
_____
_____
_____
_____

Although the two of you may agree on the essentials, there may still be some other doctrinal points on which you do not agree. Of course, no two Christians are going to agree on every point of doctrine, but you need to make certain that any difference in doctrinal opinion that the two of you have will not be enough to cause resentment and anger. So it would be a good idea to dig deeper into the religious issue. The next set of questions will help you to do just that.

- *Beliefs about Salvation*

Are both of you really Christians/saved? What is your definition of being a Christian? What is your significant other's definition of being a Christian? If one of you is not saved, then the two of you should stop dating.

_____

_____

_____

_____

_____

_____

_____

The Bible teaches us that we will have a pretty good idea as to who is saved, and who is not saved, by the fruits they produce (the behaviors they exhibit).

Although we really shouldn't judge the salvation of another, we shouldn't ignore certain red flags either. Galatians 5:22-24 says, *"the fruit of the Spirit is love, joy, peace, patience, kindness, goodness, faithfulness, gentleness and self-control. Against such things there is no law. Those who belong to Christ Jesus have crucified the sinful nature with its passions and desires."* (NIV)

Jesus said, *"Beware of false prophets who come disguised as harmless sheep, but are really wolves that will tear you apart. You can detect them by the way they act, just as you can identify a tree by its fruit. You don't pick grapes from thornbushes, or figs from thistles. A healthy tree produces good fruit, and an unhealthy tree produces bad fruit. A good tree can't produce bad fruit, and a bad tree can't produce good fruit. So every tree that does not produce good fruit is chopped down and thrown into the fire. Yes, the way to identify a tree or a person is by the kind of fruit that is produced."* (Matthew 7:15-20 NLT).

Is your significant other loving, joyful, peaceful, patient, kind, good, faithful, gentle, and self-controlled? Is he or she producing "good fruit?" If not, why not?

The Bible also teaches us that people who practice sin (without remorse and with no intentions of stopping) will not inherit the kingdom of God. In other words, they may say that they're saved but they're really not. And how they behave gives them away. Galatians 5:19-21 attests to this. It reads, *"When you follow the desires of your sinful nature, your lives will produce these evil results: sexual immorality, impure thoughts, eagerness for sinful pleasure, idolatry, participation in demonic activities, hostility, quarreling, jealousy, outbursts of anger, selfish ambition, divisions, the feeling that everyone is wrong except those in your own little group, envy, drunkenness, wild parties, and other kinds of sin. Let me tell you again, as I have before, that anyone living that sort of life will not inherit the Kingdom of God."* (NLT)

Does your significant other exhibit any of the behaviors listed in the above passage of scripture? If so, which ones? If so, is he or she comfortable with the behavior or trying to stop?

Does either one of you believe you can lose your salvation? If not, why not? If so, why?

_____

_____

_____

Does either one of you believe that a person who does not speak in tongues is not saved? If so, how has the one that believes this come to this conclusion and how does the other of you feel about this?

_____

_____

_____

Does either one of you believe that speaking in tongues is the only sign that shows that a person has been indwelled with the Holy Spirit of God? If so, how has the one that believes this come to this conclusion and how does the other of you feel about this?

_____

_____

_____

_____

_____

Do the two of you agree on the meaning of baptism?

_____

_____

_____

Does either one of you believe that human beings can be Gods, "as God," or "little gods"?

_____

_____

_____

How do both of you feel about?

- The Word Faith Movement (the leaders of this movement erroneously teach that sickness is caused by not having enough faith in God, that all Christians should have loads of money, that Christians can call things that are not into existence, and that Christians are "gods"),
- Jehovah's Witnesses (they deny that Jesus is the second person of the Godhead, that he is God),
- Mormons (they believe in three Gods, that certain men will become Gods when they die and go to heaven, and that these men will be able to have many wives in heaven),
- Unity (the leaders of this movement believe that God is a principle, not a person and that the Krishna of the Hindu is the same as Jesus)
- Christian Science (the leaders of this movement teach that Christ is a divine idea and that everything is God).

_____

_____

_____

_____

_____

_____

How do both of you feel about world religions such as Islam, Hinduism, Judaism, etc?

_____

_____

_____

How do both of you define a cult? Name some? Do each of you include Jehovah's Witnesses on your list of cults? Is there a group that one of you has included that the other one has not?

_____
_____
_____
_____
_____
_____

How do both of you interpret the following verse of scripture and what does it mean to both of you? ...

"Wives submit to your husbands as to the Lord. For the husband is the head of the wife as Christ is the head of the church, his body, of which he is the Savior. Now as the church submits to Christ, so also wives should submit to their husbands in everything." (Ephesians 5:22-24 NIV)

_____
_____
_____
_____
_____
_____

Does the man in the relationship believe that God will not instruct a wife to do anything unless God comes to her husband about it first?

_____
_____
_____

How do both of you interpret the following verse of scripture and what does it mean to both you?...

"Husbands, love your wives, just as Christ loved the church and gave himself up for her..." (Ephesians 5:25 NIV)

_____

_____

_____

_____

_____

_____

How do both of you interpret the following verse of scripture and what does it mean to both you?

"Husbands, in the same way be considerate as you live with your wives, and treat them with respect as the weaker partner and as heirs with you of the gracious gift of life, so that nothing will hinder your prayers." (1 Peter 3:7 NIV)

_____

_____

_____

_____

_____

_____

What is your definition of heresy? What is your significant other's definition of heresy?

_____

_____

_____

What religion does your significant other's mother, father, siblings etc., follow? If different from Christianity, how do you think this might affect you if you eventually marry your significant other?

_____

_____

_____

What religion does your mother, father, siblings, etc., aspire to? If different from Christianity, how do you think their beliefs might affect your marital relationship if you were to eventually marry your significant other?

_____

_____

_____

What religion does your significant other's children aspire to? If different from Christianity, how will you handle the religious differences between you and them?

_____

_____

_____

If there is a particular point of doctrine that the two of you don't agree on? Can the two of you agree to disagree as long as both of you on are on the same page when it comes to the essential doctrines of the Christian faith?

_____

_____

_____

• *Church Membership and Attendance*

Do both of you attend church? If not, why not? If so, how often do the two of you attend?

_____

_____

_____

If both of you are attending church, do the two of you attend the same church? If not, why not? Where do you attend? Where does your significant other attend?

_____

_____

_____

Do both of you feel that it is necessary for the two of you to attend the same church once you are married? If so, why? If not, why not?

_____

_____

_____

If you get married, will the two of you be attending church together? If not, why not? If so, what church will the two of you be attending?

_____

_____

_____

If the two of you decide to attend the same church, what will be the deciding factor for selecting a church?

_____

_____

_____

If the two of you decide to attend the same church, will *both of you* be satisfied and feel that you're getting the proper spiritual nourishment at that church? If not, why not?

_____

_____

_____

If you decide to attend separate churches, how will this affect the relationship between the two of you?

_____

_____

_____

What are you and your significant other's understanding of Proverbs 31:10-31? And in what way, if any, do you think your understanding of the passage of scripture will impact your relationship if the two of you get married?

_____

_____

_____

_____

_____

_____

What are you and your significant other's understanding of the book of Song of Solomon? And in what way, if any, do you think your understanding of this book of the Bible will impact your relationship if the two of you get married?

_____

_____

_____

_____

_____

_____

If you and your significant other have discovered that you could not get through this chapter without a lot of bickering then count your blessings that the two of you have discovered how incompatible you are in the area of religion and prepare to go your separate ways. However, if you and your significant other have gotten through this chapter together feeling pretty confident that you agree on the essential doctrines of the Christian faith, and that any disagreement that the two of you may have regarding other biblical doctrines that are important (but are not necessarily essential to salvation) will not be enough to hurt your relationship, then you may progress to the next chapter.

3.

LIFESTYLE

Most people get married without really thinking about the lifestyle they lead and how one's individual lifestyle can affect or be affected by the onset of a marital relationship. Anyone who marries must adjust his or her lifestyle in some way. Both husband and wife must be willing to compromise and change his or her way of doing things in order to appease and satisfy a spouse.

However, serious problems can arise when two individual lifestyles are extremely different and at opposite ends of the spectrum. And as Christians, if we marry someone with an extremely dissimilar lifestyle than ourselves, there is no question that whatever ministry the Lord has directed us in could be negatively effected. There are certain lifestyle polarities that when mixed together in a marriage can create confusion and cause great distress for both partners. Some styles of life are a result of embedded personalities. Personality is difficult to change without the help of the Lord. Therefore, how one lives his or her life is equally difficult to change. We're going to take a look at some lifestyle differences that can really hurt a marriage if neither partner is willing to substantially compromise or if one partner is routinely expected to change while the other refuses to change or only compromises very little.

- *Holy Living vs. Carnality*

There's not much compromising here. If one of you is an immature Christian (living carnally) and the other is a mature Christian (living holy), then there's sure to be conflict between the two of you because immature Christians lead sinful lives. Therefore, it is difficult to distinguish them from those who are unsaved. The following scripture passage confirms this. It reads, *"Dear brothers and sisters, when I was with you I couldn't talk to you as I would to mature Christians. I had to talk as though you belonged to this world or as though you were infants in the Christian life. I had to feed you with milk and not with solid food, because you couldn't handle anything stronger. And you still aren't ready, for you are still controlled by your own sinful desires. You are jealous of one another and quarrel with each other. Doesn't that prove you are controlled by your own desires? You are acting like people who don't belong to the Lord."* (1ˢᵗ Corinthians 3:1-3 NLT).

The mature Christian will be negatively effected by the sinful living of the Christian who has not yet reached spiritual maturity. Arguments, resentment, and disagreements will most definitely ensue if these things have not ensued already. Worse yet, the mature Christian would more than likely be influenced to engage in some of the behaviors in which the immature Christian engages in (as opposed to the other way around). 1ˢᵗ Corinthians 15:33 warns us that this is indeed the case. It reads, *"Do not be misled: 'Bad company corrupts good character.'"* It is therefore best not to continue in a relationship with someone who is not living a holy life. 1ˢᵗ Corinthians 5:11 also confirms this (as quoted in the previous chapter) and it reads, *"But now I am writing you that you must not associate with anyone who calls himself a brother but is sexually immoral or greedy, an idolater or a slanderer, a drunkard, or a swindler. With such a man do not even eat."* (NIV)

What does holy living mean to both of you? What does being a carnal Christian mean to both of you?

_____

_____

_____

_____

_____

_____

Is either one of you struggling with a particular sin that you just can't seem to shake, but you're trying to? If so, what sin/sins are both of you struggling with? What are both of you doing to overcome?

_____

_____

_____

Is either one of you struggling with a sin that you are not yet ready to give up? If so, what is the sin and why aren't you (or your significant other) willing to give it up?

_____

_____

_____

• *Ministry*

Is either one of you involved in ministry of any kind? If so, what is it? How heavily involved are you in your ministry and how would your involvement in this ministry affect a marital relationship?

_____

_____

_____

_____

_____

_____

How heavily is your significant other involved in his or her ministry?

_____

_____

_____

_____

_____

Does the ministry that you are involved in require you to be away a lot (this does not necessarily mean away from home because a person can be at home and still be away from other household members by being in a different room with the door closed)? If so, in what way and how do you think this will affect a marriage?

_____

_____

_____

Do you agree with, and are you supportive of, the ministry or ministries that your significant other is involved in? If not, why not?

_____

_____

_____

Does your significant other agree with and is he or she supportive of the ministry/ministries that you are involved in? If not, why not?

_____

_____

_____

Do you expect your significant other to slow down in his or her ministry if the two of you get married? If so, why would you want him or her to slow down and how does he or she feel about this?

_____

_____

_____

In order to be involved in the ministry that you are involved in, what sacrifices are you making (as it relates to time, money, home, friends, family, etc)? Is your significant other willing to make those same sacrifices and/or to accept the sacrifices you are already making?

_____
_____
_____
_____
_____
_____

In order for your significant other to be involved in the ministry that he or she is involved in, what sacrifices, if any, is he or she making? Are you willing to make those same sacrifices and/or to accept the sacrifices already being made?

_____
_____
_____
_____
_____
_____

• *Neatness vs. Untidiness*

If a husband and wife are at odds in this area, it can cause great tension in their marriage. Lots of people are "neat-freaks" and don't know it or won't acknowledge it. They are on the extreme end of being neat and want every little thing in place, which can feel very imposing to an untidy person. On the other hand, there are other people who are sloppy around the house and feel that those who live in the house with them should simply learn to live with it. But, neat people feel ill-at-ease living in a sloppy environment, and such an environment itself can therefore feel very imposing to them as well.

If these two lifestyles marry, then there is bound to be resentment on both sides. The one who is untidy will resent the constant nagging of the one who is neater, and the one who is neater will resent what he or she perceives as being forced to live in an environment that is uncomfortable for him or her. If both partners are not willing to compromise, there will always be a certain amount of tension in the home over this. This can be such a sore point in a marriage that both parties should be willing to compromise. The untidy person should be willing to change his or her behavior in at least a few areas and the tidy person should "let up" a little. Both partners must understand that neither one of them will change completely. Therefore they both must learn to except *improvement* from the other and not to expect a total 360-degree change.

But most people are not very willing to change or compromise when it comes to this because both sides feel they have the right to be as they are and to change would not only mean changing one's behavior, but changing one's frame of mind, which is a very difficult thing to do indeed. Therefore, if you are a very neat person (don't act as if you aren't, if you are) then it would be a good idea to pop in on your significant other unexpectedly at least twice during the course of your dating in order to get a true idea of how he or she lives. And if you're a very untidy person (don't act as if you aren't, if you are), you should be very honest with your significant other about this because although you might try very hard to change, old habits are very hard to break.

If any of the following applies to you, you might be a neat-freak:

- There absolutely must be a coaster under every glass or cup that is sat down for drinking.
- There can be no dishes in the sink...ever.
- The bed must always be made.
- All papers must be put away.
- There can never be any clothes lying around.

- Everything must be in its "proper" place (of course, that "proper" place is always defined by you).
- Other people in the house see you as a nag.

If any of the following applies to you, you might be a slob:
- You leave drinking glasses and cups all over the house.
- There are always dishes in the sink.
- The bed is *not* made more often than it is.
- Loose papers lay on tables for days.
- There are always clothes lying around.
- Food stays out overnight and crumbs are on the floor.
- Other people in the house are constantly cleaning up after you.

Define neatness. How neat are you? How neat is your significant other?

_____

_____

_____

_____

_____

_____

What is your definition of a tidy environment? An untidy environment? Does your significant other agree with your definitions?

_____

_____

_____

_____

_____

_____

What is your significant other's definition of a tidy environment? An untidy environment? Do you agree with his or her definitions?

_____

_____

_____

_____

_____

_____

How tidy do you keep your environment (where you live, your car, your workspace, etc)? Is how it's kept acceptable to your significant other?

_____

_____

_____

How tidy does your significant other keep his or her environment? Is how it's kept acceptable to you?

_____

_____

_____

How neat do you want your significant other to be?

_____

_____

_____

How neat does your significant other want you to be?

_____

_____

_____

- *Clean vs. Unclean*

Being clean is different from being neat. Being neat means everything has to be in order. Being clean means everything has to be "spic and span." The two often go hand in hand but not necessarily. And in the same way, being unclean is different from being untidy. There are many people who are neat but are not necessarily clean and there are many people who are untidy but are not necessarily unclean. For instance, people who are untidy might leave dishes in the sink for a period of days, but they may have rinsed the dishes before hand. However, people who are not clean might leave *dirty* dishes in the sink for days. There's a difference.

What does cleanliness mean to you?

_____
_____
_____
_____
_____
_____

Does your significant other agree with your definition of cleanliness? If so, in what way? If not, why not?

_____
_____
_____
_____
_____
_____

What is your significant other's definition of cleanliness?

_____
_____
_____

Do you agree with his or her definition of cleanliness? If so, in what way? If not, why not?

_____
_____
_____
_____
_____
_____

How clean do you keep your environment (where you live, your car, your workspace, etc)? Is how it's kept acceptable to your significant other?

_____
_____
_____

How clean does your significant other keep his or her environment? Is how it's kept acceptable to you?

_____
_____
_____

What is your definition of a dirty environment? Does your significant other agree with your definition? If not, why not?

_____
_____
_____

_____

_____

_____

What is your significant other's definition of a dirty environment? Do you agree with his or her definition? If not, why not?

_____

_____

_____

_____

_____

_____

* *Night person vs. Day person*

Christians who are dating should not be spending nights together because to do so could lead to premarital sex, is an appearance of evil, and decreases their credibility as a Christians. However, the two of you still need to be aware of this part of each other's lifestyle.

How late do you stay up? How late does your significant other stay up?

_____

_____

_____

If you're a night person, will you expect your significant other to stay up with you?

_____

_____

_____

If your significant other is a night person will he or she expect you to stay up?

_____

_____

_____

When you or your significant other stay up late at night, does either one of you make a lot of noise (watch television, sing, listen to the radio, etc)?

_____

_____

_____

Is either one of you a light sleeper? If so, which one of you?

_____

Does either one of you need a "quiet house" in order to get a good night's sleep? If so, how would that affect the other?

_____

_____

_____

Does either one of you need a little noise to help you sleep (i.e. the running of a fan, the radio on low)? If so, how would that affect the other?

_____

_____

_____

How early do you get up? How early does your significant other get up?

_____

_____

_____

Will you expect your significant other to get up when you get up? If so, why? Will your significant other expect you to get up when he or she gets up? If so, why?

_____

_____

_____

• *Eating Habits*

Eating habits are a big deal in a marriage because how often the husband eats, what he likes to eat, how much he likes to eat, when he likes to eat, and so forth, usually has a direct effect on how often the wife will be cooking (unless of course, the husband cooks too).

How often do you eat? How often does your significant other eat?

_____

_____

_____

Is either one of you a "picky" eater? What do you refuse to eat (i.e. leftovers, TV dinners, fast foods, meat, fish, poultry, canned food, packaged food, sweets, etc)? What does your significant other refuse to eat?

_____

_____

_____

Is either one of you a vegetarian? If so, how would this affect the two of you if you were to get married?

_____

_____

_____

• **Other Habits**

Does either one of you smoke? If so, how much and when? If so, how do you think this will affect the two of you were you to get married? Does the one who smokes, plan on quitting?

_____

_____

_____

Does either one of you drink? If so, how much and when? Have you or has your significant other ever been drunk? If so, when was the last time this drunkenness occurred? How often has this drunkenness occurred?

_____

_____

_____

Does either one of you gamble? If so, how much and when? Has either one of you ever gambled when you could not afford to? Does either one of you have any gambling debts? Has either one of you ever participated in Gamblers Anonymous or considered doing so?

_____

_____

_____

Does either one of you have any other habits that you need to tell your significant other about? If so, what are they and how do you think these habits will affect your relationship if the two of you get married?

_____

_____

_____

Do either of you have any habits that the other finds annoying? If so, what are they?

_____

_____

_____

• *Health*

Your health and wellbeing have a great impact on your lifestyle, which will have a great impact on your marriage.

Are both of you in good health? If not, explain.

_____

_____

_____

Is either one of you allergic to anything? If so, what?

_____

_____

_____

Are both of you physically fit? If not, explain.

_____

_____

_____

Do you have a regular schedule at the gym? If so, does your significant other? If your significant other doesn't work out or go to the gym, do you think that he or she should? If you don't have a regular schedule at the gym does your significant other think you should?

_____

_____

_____

Does either one of you have any illnesses? Is either one of you on any kind of medication? If so, what's the illness? And what kind of medication is being taken?

_____

_____

_____

Does either one of you have a family history of a specific medical problem? If so what is it?

_____

_____

_____

Does either one of you have a family history of mental illness? If so, what is the specific illness?

_____

_____

_____

Does either one of you now suffer from or has ever suffered from a mental illness? If so, is or was medication necessary? If medication is involved, is it being taken as prescribed? If not, why not? Is or has counseling been involved?

_____

_____

_____

Has either one of you ever been committed to a mental health hospital or institute? If so, what were the circumstances that led to institutionalization? Has either one of you ever been treated for mental illness on an outpatient basis? If so, expound.

_____

_____

_____

Has either one of you ever received any other kind of mental health or counseling services? If so, expound. Has the problem been resolved?

_____

_____

_____

_____

_____

_____

Is the woman in the relationship prone to severe menstrual cramps, pre-menstrual syndrome (which may include depression, irritability, bloating, fatigue, weight gain, etc), or any other "female problems?" If so, what are the problems and how do they affect the two of you? How do the two of you feel about these problems?

_____

_____

_____

Does either one of you snore? If so, how will it affect the other?

_____

_____

_____

• **Hobbies and other Activities**

Does either one of you have any hobbies? If so, what kind of hobbies?

_____

_____

_____

Are both of you interested in the same hobbies?

_____

_____

_____

How much do your hobbies cost to maintain? How much does your significant other's hobbies cost to maintain? Are your hobbies or the hobbies of your significant other expensive? If so, how expensive?

_____

_____

_____

Do your hobbies or the hobbies of your significant other take up a lot of space? A lot of time? If so, in what way?

_____

_____

_____

Is one of you involved in a hobby in which it would be difficult to include the other? If so, why and how does the other one feel about this?

_____

_____

_____

Does either one of you have a "loner" hobby (i.e. playing solitude, reading, etc.)?

_____

_____

_____

Are there any other activities that either of you are involved in that takes up quite a bit of time (i.e. College student, Book club, sports activities, etc.)?

_____

_____

_____

- ***Vacation***

What does taking a vacation mean to you? To your significant other?

_____

_____

_____

Are you or your significant other someone who likes to get up and go a lot? If so, in what way?

_____

_____

_____

Do you like to travel? If so, where (within the country? Out of the country)? Does your significant other like to travel? If so, where?

_____

_____

_____

Are you a "homebody?" Is your significant other a "homebody?" If so, in what way?

_____

_____

_____

- ***Outdoor person vs. Indoor***

Do you like hiking, the beach, picnicking, fishing, camping, etc., or would you rather stay indoors? What about your significant other? Does he or she prefer the outdoors or the indoors?

_____

_____

_____

- *Pets*

Do you have any pets? If so, how does your significant other feel about your pet/pets? If you don't have a pet, do you want one? If so, what kind of pet and how does your significant other feel about you having a pet?

_____

_____

_____

Does your significant other have pets? If so, how do you feel about his or her pet/pets? If not, does your significant other want a pet? If so, what kind of pet does he or she want and how would you feel about your significant other having a pet?

_____

_____

_____

Is there any kind of pet that either of you would absolutely be opposed to having? If so, what kind and why?

_____

_____

_____

Is either one of you allergic to animals?

_____

_____

_____

- *Living environment*

What is it that each of you would absolutely not be able to live with when it comes to the décor of your home?

_____

_____

_____

How do you feel about having pictures of family members or friends placed in the house? How does your significant other feel about this?

_____

_____

_____

Are there any pictures of anybody in particular that you or your significant other would not want placed in your home?

_____

_____

_____

What colors do you like? What colors does your significant other like?

_____

_____

_____

What colors don't you like? What colors doesn't your significant other like?

_____
_____
_____

What kind of art do you like? Don't you like? What kind of art does your significant other like? Not like?

_____
_____
_____
_____
_____
_____

What kind of furniture do you like? Don't you like? What kind of furniture does your significant other like? Not like?

_____
_____
_____
_____
_____
_____

Do you move the furniture around frequently or do you like it to stay where it is? What about your significant other? Does he or she move the furniture around frequently?

_____
_____
_____

Assuming that you are not living together (and you shouldn't be if both of you are Christians) what kind of home do each of you live in (house, apartment, condominium, etc)? What kind of home would each of you prefer to live in?

_____

_____

_____

Does either one of you live with anyone? If so, who and why?

_____

_____

_____

What kind of neighborhood do you think you would be most comfortable living in? What kind of neighborhood are you absolutely not willing to live in?

_____

_____

_____

What kind of neighborhood would your significant other be most comfortable living in? What kind of neighborhood is he or she absolutely not willing to live in?

_____

_____

_____

Does either one of you already live in a neighborhood in which the other is absolutely not willing to live in?

_____

_____

_____

Do you like a cool house or a warm house? Does your significant other like a cool house or a warm house?

_____

_____

_____

Would you prefer to live in the city or the country? Would your significant other prefer to live in the city or the country?

_____

_____

_____

Does either one of you feel that you need to live close to your parents, or to another family member? If so, why? How does the other of you feel about this?

_____

_____

_____

Does either one of you have any plans or desires to eventually move far away from where you are currently residing? If so, where would you like to live and why?

_____

_____

_____

Would either of you like to relocate to a place that is vastly different from where you are residing now? If so, where would you like to live and why?

_____

_____

_____

• *Telephone habits*

Do you like talking on the phone to your significant other or would you rather talk to him or her in person? Does your significant other like talking to you on the phone or would he or she rather talk to you in person?

How often do you talk on the phone with friends and/or family? How often does your significant other talk on the phone with friends and/or family?

How does your significant other feel about you talking on the phone to other people? How do you feel about your significant other talking on the phone to other people?

Does either one of you feel that phone conversations with family and friends should be limited to a certain time of the day or have a time limit? If so, what time of the day is off limits? How long is too long for a telephone conversation?

Is there someone that your significant other is associated with that you absolutely do not want him or her to spend a long time speaking to on the phone? If so, who is it and why the limitation?

_____

_____

_____

- ***Entertainment and Relaxation***

What kind of entertainment do you like? What kind of entertainment does your significant other like?

_____

_____

_____

What kind of entertainment don't you like? What kind of entertainment doesn't your significant other like?

_____

_____

_____

What kind of entertainment are you absolutely opposed to? Is your significant other absolutely opposed to?

_____

_____

_____

How do each of you like to spend your leisure time?

_____

_____

_____

Does either one of you nap during the day? If so, is that all right with the other one?

_____

_____

_____

- **Holiday Expectations**

Where and with whom do you spend Thanksgiving / Christmas?

_____

_____

_____

Where and with whom does your significant other spend Thanksgiving / Christmas?

_____

_____

_____

How much money do each of you spend at Christmas and on whom?

_____

_____

_____

_____

_____

_____

What do each of you do for the 4th of July, Memorial Day, Labor Day, etc? What do you expect the other to do during these holidays? The Christmas holidays? Thanksgiving?

_____
_____
_____
_____
_____
_____

• *Personal Space*

How much time to yourself do you need? How much time does your significant other need to himself or herself?

_____
_____
_____

How much personal space are you willing to give to your significant other? How much personal space is he or she willing to give to you?

_____
_____
_____

• *Other things to consider*

Is either of you a "couch potato?" If so, how does your significant other feel about this? How often do each of you like to look at television?

_____
_____
_____

Does either one of you like watching sports on television? If so, when, where, and how long in a given day? How does your significant other feel about this?

_____

_____

_____

If both of you have answered all of these questions honestly, then the two of you should be able to determine whether or not your lifestyles are compatible. Of course, you will not be one hundred percent compatible in every lifestyle area. But if there is even one area where the two of you differ so greatly that there is no hope for compromise and you know this difference could be a serious detriment to your relationship if you were to get married, then it's time to really take a hard look at whether or not you should continue dating. However, if you feel good about your lifestyle compatibility or if you at least feel that the two of you will be able to compromise where compromise is needed (don't say you're willing to compromise unless you really are), then you may progress to the next chapter.

4.

THE "EX" FACTOR

The majority of people who are seriously dating and thinking about marriage have dated others in the past. And many of those who are now involved in a serious relationship, have been married before. Some people have been married more than once. Things can get complicated if your significant other is still somehow tied to his or her ex-spouse, ex-fiancé, and/or ex-girlfriend/boyfriend. What usually keeps a man and a woman tied together are children, and on rare occasions, alimony, business ties, legal dealings etc. If your significant other is tied to an "ex," then you will be just as much tied to that ex if you and your significant other get married.

Furthermore, there are those who have had affections for someone in the past, but when they expressed their feelings they were rejected by the particular person who was the object of their desire. Or, maybe there was no rejection, but for some reason, things just never materialized. You want to make sure that your significant other is not dating you because you remind him or her of someone that he or she still has feelings for. And you want to make sure that you're not on the rebound from a relationship that your significant other recently had that has gone bad (be it a marriage, engagement, or just a dating relationship), or from a rejection that he or she has recently sustained.

It usually takes about a year to get over a dissolved relationship, maybe even longer. It takes a year because it takes that long to get through each important holiday, each important anniversary date, each important birthday date and so on, alone. Therefore, if your significant other has broken up with someone and a year has not yet passed, he or she might still be in the grieving process and you could very well be on the rebound. If you are on the rebound, the marriage will be in trouble from "day one" because there is no way you will be able to compete with the person your significant other is still grieving over.

The following questions should help you to determine just how much of an impact an ex-spouse, ex-girlfriend/boyfriend, ex-fiancé, or even a love interest that never materialized will have on your relationship if you marry your significant other.

• *Rebound*

Have you or has your significant other recently been involved with someone (within the last year) in which the other party dissolved the relationship against your wishes or against the wishes of your significant other? If so, what happened? And do you (or your significant other) still think about that person? If so, in what way and how does the other of you feel about this?

_____

_____

_____

_____

_____

_____

Has one of you recently made advances towards someone (within the last 6 months) but those advances were rejected? If so, what happened and do you or your significant other still think about this person?

_____

_____

_____

If you or your significant other still thinks about this person, in what way is this person still thought about and how does the other feel about this?

_____

_____

_____

_____

_____

_____

_____

* *Ex-spouses, ex-fiancés, ex-girlfriends, ex-boyfriends*

Is either one of you still legally married but separated? If so, the two of you should stop dating one another.

_____

_____

_____

Is either one of you divorced? If so, how long have you been divorced?

_____

_____

_____

If you are divorced, why are you divorced? If your significant other is divorced, why is he or she divorced?

_____

_____

_____

How does your significant other feel about the reasons why you are divorced, and/or, how do you feel about the reasons why your significant other is divorced?

_____
_____
_____

Do you still have contact with an ex? If so, why? Do you plan to continue to have contact? If so, how does your significant other feel about this and how do you think this will affect a future marriage?

_____
_____
_____
_____
_____
_____

Does your significant other still have contact with an ex? If so, why? Does he or she plan to continue having contact? If so, how do you feel about this and how do you think this will affect a future marriage? If one of you must visit an ex from time to time, for whatever reason, is it okay if the other of you comes along? If not, why not?

_____
_____
_____
_____
_____
_____

If you have an ex-spouse, how much say-so and influence does the ex-spouse have in your life? How do you and your significant other think this say-so and influence might affect your marital relationship if the two of you were to get married?

_____

_____

_____

_____

_____

_____

If your significant other has an ex-spouse, how much say-so and influence does the ex-spouse have in his or her life? How do you and your significant other think this say-so might affect the two of you if you were to get married?

_____

_____

_____

_____

_____

_____

What religion does your significant other's ex-spouse, ex-girlfriend/boyfriend, ex-fiancé (that he or she still has ties to) follow? Your significant other's child's mother? Your significant other's child's father? If different from Christianity, how do you and your significant other think this might affect your relationship if the two of you were to get married?

_____

_____

_____

_____

_____

_____

What religion does your ex-spouse, ex-girlfriend/boyfriend, ex-fiancée (that you still have ties to), follow? If different from Christianity, how do you and your significant other think this might affect your relationship if the two of you were to get married?

_____

_____

_____

Have you substantially gotten over the feelings you once had for your ex-spouse/ ex-fiancé/ ex-girlfriend or boyfriend? If not, how do you think this might affect a future marital relationship between the two of you?

_____

_____

_____

Has your ex-spouse/ ex-fiancé/ ex-girlfriend/boyfriend substantially gotten over the feelings he or she once had for you? If not, how do you think this might affect a future marital relationship between the two of you?

_____

_____

_____

Has your significant other substantially gotten over the feelings he or she once had for his or her ex-spouse/ ex-fiancé/ ex-girlfriend/boyfriend? If not, how do you think this might affect a future marital relationship between the two of you?

_____

_____

_____

Has your significant other's ex-spouse/ ex-fiancé/ ex-girlfriend/boyfriend gotten over the feelings he or she once had for your significant other? If not, how do you think this might affect a future marital relationship between the two of you?

_____

_____

_____

Does your significant other flirt with his or her ex in any way? Is he or she sexually suggestive towards his or her ex in any way? If so, in what way? How does this make you feel?

_____

_____

_____

Does your significant other's ex flirt with, or make sexually suggestive gestures/remarks towards him or her? If so, how do you feel about this? How does your significant other react to the remarks or gestures?

_____

_____

_____

Does your ex flirt with, or make sexually suggestive gestures/remarks to you? If so, how does your significant other feel about this? If so, how do you react to the remarks or gestures?

_____

_____

_____

Do you flirt with your ex or make sexually suggestive remarks/gestures towards him or her? If so, why? How does your significant other feel about this?

_____

_____

_____

Is your significant other's ex jealous of you? If so, why and in what way?

_____

_____

_____

Are you jealous of your significant other's ex? If so, why and in what way?

_____

_____

_____

Is your significant other jealous of your ex? If so, why and in what way?

_____

_____

_____

Is your ex jealous of your significant other? If so, why and in what way?

_____

_____

_____

Does either one of you have any gifts from an ex-spouse, ex-fiancé/ ex-girlfriend / ex-boyfriend, or a non-related member of the opposite sex that you are holding on to? (i.e. wedding rings, love poems, jewelry, mementos, art, photographs, etc.) If so, what are they and why are you holding on to these things? If so, how does your significant other feel about you holding on to these things?

_____

_____

_____

_____

_____

_____

Does either one of you compare the other to an ex-spouse, ex-fiancé, or ex-girlfriend/boyfriend? If so, in what way and why? How does the one who has been compared feel about being compared?

_____

_____

_____

No ex-spouse, ex-girlfriend, ex-boyfriend, ex-fiancé, or ex-love interest should be able to exert control and negative influence in your household. If either of you believe that an ex could cause problems in your marriage, then the one with the ex has to be willing to set and enforce boundaries when it comes to the ex. Furthermore, what the ex wants should never come before what the current spouse wants. The current spouse must come first. If one of you is not willing to put the other before an ex, then a marriage between the two of you will probably be doomed. However, if you both agree that certain boundaries will be set and adhered to when it comes to the ex and if both of you agree as to what those boundaries are, then you may progress to the next chapter.

5.

FAMILY AND FRIENDS

How a person gets along with his or her family and friends is a great indicator of how well that person will get along with you. Therefore it is important to investigate. You also need to know whether or not there are people in your significant other's life who might cause a problem in your marriage if the two of you were to get "tie the knot."

- *Family*

How large is your family? How large is your significant other's family?

_____

_____

_____

Has your significant other met members of your family? If not, why not? If so, are there any members of your family that your significant other does not particularly care for or does not get along with? If so, why? And how will this affect the two of you if you get married?

_____

_____

_____

Have you met your significant other's family members? If not, why not? If so, are there any members of his or her family that you do not particularly care for or that you don't get along with? If not, why not? And how will this affect the two of you if you get married?

_____

_____

_____

How many brothers and sisters do you have and what is the order of your birth (first born, middle child, youngest child)? How many brothers and sisters does your significant other have and what is the order of his or her birth?

_____

_____

_____

If you have brothers and sisters, describe your relationship with them and how you think that relationship may affect you and your significant other?

_____

_____

_____

_____

_____

_____

If your significant other has brothers and sisters, what kind of a relationship does he or she have with them and how do you think that relationship might affect the two of you?

_____

_____

_____

_____

_____

_____

Is there anyone in your family that you don't particularly get along with? If there is, who is it and why don't you? To what extent don't you get along with this family member?

_____

_____

_____

_____

_____

_____

Is there anyone in your significant other's family that he or she doesn't particularly get along with? If there is, who is it and why the disdain? To what extent is the tension between the two of them?

_____

_____

_____

_____

_____

_____

Does your significant other have any family members that he or she is close to that are not Christians? Do you? If so, how do you think this will affect the two of you if you get married?

_____

_____

_____

Are you close to anyone in your family, in particular, that you see often and talk to a lot? If so, who is it and how does your significant other feel about this?

_____

_____

_____

Is your significant other close to anyone in his or her family, in particular, that he or she sees often or talks to a lot? If so, who is it and how do you feel about this?

_____

_____

_____

Does either one of you have a family member who drops by the house often or who you visit often? If so, who is it? How does your significant other feel about this? How do you feel about this?

_____

_____

_____

Describe the type of relationship you have with your parents (if they are still living) or had with them (if they are deceased). If your parents are living, how much of an influence do your parents have over you and in what ways?

_____

_____

_____

Describe the type of relationship your significant other has or had with his or her parents. And if his or her parents are living, how much of an influence do they have over him or her and in what ways?

_____

_____

_____

Is either one of you estranged from your parents or from one of your parents in any way? If so, why? How would this estrangement affect a future marital relationship?

_____

_____

_____

How will the relationship you have or had with your parents affect a future marital relationship?

_____

_____

_____

How will the relationship your significant other has or had with his or her parents affect a future marital relationship?

_____

_____

_____

Have your parents expressed a dislike of your significant other or has your significant other's parents expressed a dislike of you? If so, why? How do you think this sort of thing will affect a marital relationship between you and your significant other?

_____

_____

_____

Is either one of you a "Mama's boy," or "Daddy's girl?" If so, in what way?

_____

_____

_____

Does either one of you have a relative (or a friend) that you would describe as a freeloader? If so, how close are you or your significant other to this relative? Do you or does your significant other help this relative out a lot? If so, how? And how would this affect your relationship if the two of you were to get married?

_____

_____

_____

_____

_____

_____

If your significant other has expressed to you that other people in his or her life will come before you, are you willing to accept this? How does this make you feel?

_____

_____

_____

Do you or does your significant other have any close association with family members that are involved in any kind of illegal activities, have trouble with the law, or have any problems with drugs, alcohol, gambling, domestic violence, finances, their marriages, etc? If so, who are these family members and how close are you or is your significant other to them? How might this close affiliation affect the two of you if you were to get married?

_____

_____

_____

Does either one of you *often* attend, organize, or become involved in family reunions? If so, to what extent is your involvement?

_____

_____

_____

Does either one of you have families that practice unusual family traditions? If so, what are they and how would the practicing of these traditions affect the two of you if you were to get married?

_____

_____

_____

Do both of you believe in putting your spouse above all others (except God of course)? If so, does this include putting your spouse above your children and other family members? If not, why not? Who would come before your spouse?

_____

_____

_____

• *Friends*

How many close friends do both of you have? Who are they? Have you met each other's friends? If not, why not? Do both of you approve of each other's friends? If not, why not?

_____

_____

_____

_____

_____

_____

_____

Does either one of you have close platonic friends of the opposite sex? If so, what do these friendships entail? Does either one of you intend to maintain these friendships if you should ever get married? If so, how does the other feel about this?

_____

_____

_____

How important is it to each of you to maintain the same intensity of friendship that you have with your friends of the opposite sex? If it is very important, why is it important? If it is not important, why is it not important?

_____

_____

_____

_____

_____

_____

Who does each of you want to remain close to and why? Name names. Have either of you had sex with any of these people in the past?

_____

_____

_____

_____

_____

_____

How *acceptable* is it to you for your significant other to have close friends of the opposite sex and maintain those friendships? How *acceptable* is it to him or her for you to have close friends of the opposite sex and maintain those friendships? What would make it unacceptable?

_____

_____

_____

_____

_____

_____

Is either one of you jealous of any friend or familial relationship that the other has? If so, who is the jealousy pointed at and why?

_____

_____

_____

Does either one of you have a friend or friends who are homosexual? If so, explain. How does the other one feel about the friendship?

_____

_____

_____

Does either one of you have friends or associates that the other one is not particularly fond of? If so, how do the two of you think this may affect a marital relationship?

_____

_____

_____

If you have friends that your significant other does not approve of and you are not willing to give up these friends, then the two of you may have grave problems if you marry one another. The same applies if your significant other has friends that you disapprove of whom he or she is not willing to give up. However, it's different when it comes to family members. It is very difficult to break a family tie. And although the Bible says that we are to leave mother and father to cling to our spouses, putting our spouses first before family members often proves a difficult task for many of us.

It is essential, therefore, to make certain that both of you believe that one's husband or one's wife comes first before anyone else, besides God of course. The Bible confirms this when it teaches that a man and a woman who marry one another become one flesh and that a man should leave his father and mother and cling to his wife (Genesis 2:24). If just one of you is having a difficult time making this proclamation then you might want to reconsider taking things further, because it is inevitable that family issues will plague your marriage. However, if both of you agree that the other comes first, and if both of you are comfortable with each other's friends and family, then you may progress to the next chapter.

6.

CHILDREN

One of the essential ingredients of a good marriage is agreement by both partners when it comes to the rearing of their children. If a husband and wife are at odds about the children, the marital home is a very unpleasant place indeed. In addition to this, there are many married couples who never discussed, before they were married, how many children either of them wanted and whether or not they wanted children at all. It is not wise to marry someone who doesn't want children if you do, or, who wants children if you don't. Nor is it wise to marry someone who wants significantly more children than you do, or vise versa.

This area of concern cannot be taken lightly. People who want children really want them...badly. And people who don't want children *don't want them* just as badly. Having a child is a lifetime thing. It is a forever thing. There's no going back. Therefore it is absolutely imperative that the two of you find out where each of you stand on the issue. If you really don't want children but you know that your significant other does, don't hold back this information hoping that he or she will change his or her mind once the two of you are married. Chances are, he or she won't. And if you really want children and you know that your significant other doesn't, make sure to be honest with your significant other and let him or her know that you really want children.

There are those who want children who knowingly marry someone who doesn't. They've entered into the marriage hoping that their marriage partner will change his or her mind. And some even plot to trick the new spouse into having children. This kind of thing can devastate a marital union and is really unfair to the person who went into the marriage thinking that there was an agreement not to have children.

- *How many?*

Do you want to have children? If so, how many and when? If not, why not? If so, why?

_____

_____

_____

Does your significant other want to have children? If so, how many and when? If not, why not? If so, why?

_____

_____

_____

If you would like to have more than one child, how far apart do you want your children to be? How far apart does your significant other want the children to be?

_____

_____

_____

Has either one of you given any children up for adoption? If so, what were the circumstances behind relinquishing your parental rights? Do you intend to ever make contact with the child or children you have given up?

_____

_____

_____

Would either of you ever consider adopting a child? If so, under what circumstances would you want to adopt a child and how would your significant other feel about this?

_____

_____

_____

Would either of you ever want to become a foster parent? If so, under what circumstances would you want to become a foster parent and how would your significant other feel about this?

_____

_____

_____

- *Child care*

If the two of you decide to have children, which one of you will be the primary caretaker of the children and why?

_____

_____

_____

If the wife is working, will she go back to work after having the baby? If so, when? If not, why not? If she goes back to work, are both of you in agreement with the length of time she'd be off work?

_____

_____

_____

If both of you are working, what will the child care arrangements be? If a relative, will this relative want to baby-sit or is it assumed that this relative will automatically tend to this duty without question? Is it felt that this relative *should* tend to this duty?

_____

_____

_____

Are there any children or "adult children" in your life or in the life
of your significant other that either of you have a parental
relationship with, but who are not children of yours or your
significant other's biologically (i.e. step children from a previous
marriage, God-children, nieces, nephews, etc)? If so, what kind of
relationship do you have with them? How does your significant
other feel about the relationship you have with them?

_____

_____

_____

_____

_____

_____

- **Child rearing**

Do the two of you agree on child rearing practices? If not, what
are the differences?

_____

_____

_____

Do the two of you agree on how children should be disciplined? If
not, how do the two of you differ?

_____

_____

_____

If the two of you were to have children, would you want to send them to a private school? If so, how does your significant other feel about this? Would your significant other want to send the children to a private school? If so, how do you feel about this?

_____

_____

_____

Would you want your children to be home-schooled? If not, why not? If so, who would do it? Would your significant other want the children to be home-schooled? If not, why not? If so, who does he or she think should do it?

_____

_____

_____

Would you want your baby to be breast-fed? If not, why not? If so, why? Would your significant other want the baby to be breast-fed? If not, why not? If so, why?

_____

_____

_____

* *Stepchildren*

If one or both of you already have minor children, will those children be living in your home with you and your new spouse? How do both of you feel about this? Will both of you be allowed to discipline them? If not, why not? If so, in what way?

_____

_____

_____

If your stepchildren will not be living with you, will they be coming over for the weekends? Holidays? If so, who will be responsible for looking after them? Will both of you share in this responsibility? If not, why not?

_____

_____

_____

Are your to-be stepchildren currently attending private school? If so, is your significant other paying for it? If so, how do you feel about this? Would you want your stepchildren to continue their private education even if the two of you have, or will have, children of your own?

_____

_____

_____

If one of you already has minor children, who will come first, the children or the spouse?

_____

_____

_____

If one of you already has minor children, have those children met your significant other? If not, why not? If so, do the children get along with him or her? If not, why not? And if not, how do you think this will affect your relationship if the two of you were to get married?

_____

_____

_____

_____

If one of you already has minor children, do the children have any physical disabilities, illnesses, social problems, learning disabilities, behavioral problems, etc? If so, what are the difficulties that the children are experiencing and how do you think this would affect a marital relationship?

_____

_____

_____

If you already have children, how do your children get along with your significant other? How do your children feel about him or her? How does your significant other feel about your children? Will your children accept your significant other as a parental figure? How will your children refer to your significant other?

_____

_____

_____

_____

_____

_____

If your significant other already has children, how do you get along with his or her children? How do the children feel about you? How do you feel about the children? Will his or her children accept you as a parental figure? How will the children refer to you?

_____

_____

_____

_____

_____

_____

Will both of you consider the stepparent to have as equal of a parental role as the biological parent? If not, why not? How will this consideration or non-consideration work in a marriage?

_____

_____

_____

Will the stepchildren consider the stepparent to have as equal of a parental role as the biological parents? If not, why not? How will this affect a marriage?

_____

_____

_____

If both of you will be bringing minor children into a potential marriage, will these children get along with one another? If not, why not?

_____

_____

_____

Will you be able to love your stepchildren the same as you love your own children or the same *as if* they were your own children? If not, why not?

_____

_____

_____

Will your significant other be able to love your children the same as he or she loves his or her own children or the same *as if* the children were his or hers? If not, why not?

_____

_____

_____

• *Other concerns regarding children*

Are there any children whom either of you baby-sit often, even on an occasional basis (this does not pertain to your own children)? If so, how does the other feel about this?

_____

_____

_____

If you're the man in the relationship, is there a woman somewhere that says you fathered her child, but you deny it? If so, explain.

_____

_____

_____

Does the man in the relationship have a strong feeling that he may have fathered a child that he has never known? If so, with whom does he think he may have had this child? Is he willing to investigate the matter? Are you willing to let him investigate the matter? If not, why not?

_____

_____

_____

_____

_____

_____

Has the man in the relationship ever donated to a sperm bank? If so, why and what became of this?

_____

_____

_____

If you're the woman in the relationship, is there a man somewhere who you say fathered your child but he denies it? If so, explain.

_____

_____

_____

If you're the woman in the relationship have you ever been a surrogate mother or considered becoming a surrogate mother? If so, why? Do you think something like this is compatible with Christianity? How does your significant other feel about this?

_____

_____

_____

If you are the woman in the relationship, have you ever had an abortion? If so, how does your significant other feel about this?

_____

_____

_____

If you're the man in the relationship, have you ever encouraged a woman to get an abortion or have you ever paid for an abortion?

If so, how does your significant other feel about this?

_____
_____
_____

Has either one of you ever had your rights involuntarily terminated to any children you've had or taken care of? If so, what were the circumstances that led to the termination?

_____
_____
_____

Has either one of you ever been investigated for child abuse and/or neglect or had children removed from your care because of child abuse and/or neglect? If so, explain.

_____
_____
_____

Of course, as stated in the Introduction, the two of you will not agree on every point or factor. However, when it comes to the question of children, if the two of you are at opposite ends of the podium on most of the factors (number of children to have, if any, child rearing practices, child care issues, step children issues, etc) and while discussing these things you have found that neither of you are really willing to compromise much, then it would be best for the two of you not to take the relationship any further.

However, if the two of you are basically in agreement with each other on (or at least willing to compromise effectively in regard to) whether or not to have children, how many children you want, and what the dos and don'ts will be regarding the children and step-children, then you may progress to the next chapter.

7.

WORK, FINANCES, AND MONEY

During the days in which the Bible was written, it was understood in early Jewish society that a husband's main role in his marriage was to financially provide for his wife. A man did not enter into a marriage expecting his wife to work outside of the home. Moreover, the culture was such that married women had plenty of help in the home. Most married women during that time had either extended family or servants to help in the home.

However, in today's Western society, family and marriage culture is radically different from that of biblical times. Most men, including those in the church, want their wives to abide by the traditional female marital role of housekeeper and child caretaker, but do not abide by the traditional male role of sole provider themselves. They expect their wives to work outside of the home in order to take up the financial slack. Granted, many women desire to work outside of the home and many have hopes of a career. But tradition says that a married woman who works should be working because she wants to and not because she must. The passage of scripture in Proverbs 31:10-31 attests to this. And when reading those passages of scripture it can be fairly deduced that the woman depicted as virtuous in the passage was working because she wanted to and not because her husband was unable to adequately provide for her.

Despite this, it has become "incorrect" in church culture for a woman to desire that a man be able to take care of her according to her needs. Women who are willing to marry men who don't have much to offer them financially are applauded while a woman who insists that a man be able to financially take care of her is often labeled a gold digger, materialistic, and/or lacking a certain spirituality. Many men in the church often justify this way of thinking by falling back on the adage that these days, it takes two salaries to run a household. However, the expectation is not that the husband will therefore work two jobs, if need be, to bring in the necessary two salaries, but that the wife will be the one instead to work the two jobs (one inside the home and one outside the home).

In order to further justify this way of thinking, many men will turn to the passage of scripture that talks about the virtuous wife in Proverbs 31 and point out how she stayed up all night taking care of the needs of her family and worked two jobs plus took care of the house. However, they tend to overlook the fact that this virtuous wife's husband took care of her extraordinarily well and supplied her with maids and servants who were there to take care of the children and the house, while she was away tending to her career and entrepreneur business ventures. Her husband took care of her not only according to her needs, but also according to her desires and ambitions.

Keeping all of this in mind, it is essential that both the man and the woman in a relationship agree on who does what in and outside of the home. A decision must be made as to whether or not the man will be the sole financial provider or whether or not the woman will work outside of the home also, and whether or not she will do so because she wants to or because she will be expected to. If assumptions are made without discussing these things before marriage, great turmoil surrounding these issues can creep into a marriage and destroy it.

Along with considering whether or not the two of you prefer a traditional marital lifestyle (man is the sole provider), or a non-traditional marital lifestyle (the woman works and helps to support the family), it is also important for each partner to be mindful of how the other likes to spend money, of whether or not the other is for or against budgeting, of whether or not the other likes to put money into the stock market, of whether or not the other spends frugally or haphazardly, and the like.

- *Work*

If the two of you get married, who will be working, both of you or one of you? If only one of you, which one and why?

_____

_____

_____

If applicable, when do you plan to retire? Does your significant other agree with the timeline you've set for retirement? If not, why not? When does your significant other plan to retire? Do you agree with the time line he or she has set for retirement? If not, why not?

_____

_____

_____

Does either one of you believe in the traditional male role of the man being the sole financial provider for the family? If so, why? If not, why not?

_____

_____

_____

If so, does the man in the relationship make enough money to provide for the woman in a way that is acceptable to her? If not, is the woman in the relationship willing to contribute financially to the marriage to "take up the slack"?

_____

_____

_____

If so, how does the man in the relationship feel about having a working wife and how does the woman in the relationship feel about having to take up the slack?

_____

_____

_____

_____

_____

_____

If the woman is not willing to work to take up the slack, is the man in the relationship willing to work a second job in order to adequately provide for his family? If not, why not? If so, what kind of hours would he be working and how will the woman feel about him being away from the home so much?

_____

_____

_____

Do both of you work a regular "nine to five" job? If so, what kind of job do you have? What kind of job does your significant other have?

_____

_____

_____

If the woman is bringing in more financial income than the man in the relationship is, how does the man feel about this? How does the woman feel about this?

_____

_____

_____

If the two of you get married, and both of you are working outside of the home, is there any situation that could come about in which the man in the relationship would want his wife to quit her job and stay at home? If so, how does the woman in the relationship feel about this?

_____

_____

_____

Is there any situation in which the woman in the relationship would want to quit her job and stay at home? If so, how does the man in the relationship feel about this?

_____

_____

_____

Would the man in the relationship be willing to hire a maid or a nanny for his wife if both he and she are working? If not, why not? Would the man in the relationship be willing to hire a maid or a nanny even if his wife is not working? If not, why not?

_____

_____

_____

Would the man in the relationship be willing to help with the chores around the house if both he and his wife are working? If not, why not? If so, how often would he be willing to help? Would the man in the relationship be willing to help with the chores around the house even if his wife is not working?

_____

_____

_____

Is either one of you a "workaholic?" If so, in what way?

_____

_____

_____

Does either one of you work long hours? If so, how long and when?

_____

_____

_____

Does either one of you often call in sick? If so, are you really sick or is it that you just don't feel like going into work?

_____

_____

_____

Is either one of you often late getting to the job? If so, why?

_____

_____

_____

Is either one of you having trouble on the job? If so, in what way? How does the other one feel about this?

_____

_____

_____

If one or both of you are not working a "regular nine to five" is it because of one or more of the following reasons?

- You are employed by the church as your main or only source of income.
- You are self-employed or in business for yourself.
- You haven't left home.
- Someone is taking care of you.
- You are "between jobs."
- You are an artist, musician, actor, etc, trying to "make it."
- You are *living* off of a lawsuit settlement.
- You are on workman's compensation.
- You are on a leave of absence from your job.
- You have been suspended from your job.
- You are retired.
- You are rich.
- You are soon to be rich (waiting for an inheritance, the reading of a will, a lawsuit settlement, etc).
- You've been fired.
- You quit your job.
- For one reason or another, you are often considered as unemployable.
- You just graduated from college.
- You're looking for a job but haven't been able to find one.
- You don't want to work.
- You're on disability.
- You're living on alimony.
- Although you try very hard, you just can't seem to find work.
- There are certain jobs you won't do.
- You can't seem to find a *steady* job.
- Other.

If one or both of you are not working for one or more of the reasons cited above, please explain.

_____

_____

_____

If both of you are working, what will each of you expect from the other when both of you get home from work every day?

_____

_____

_____

_____

_____

_____

* *Money and Household finances*

In many states, a man making minimum wage is only making a few hundred dollars above the poverty level. If he marries a woman who has no financial income herself, then the two of them will be living *under* the poverty level with just his salary alone.

How much money do each of you make or have?

_____

_____

_____

Would either one of you want to enter into a prenuptial agreement? If so, why? If so, does the other agree?

_____

_____

_____

Who will have control of the household money if the two of you were to get married? If just one, which one of you, why, and in what way? If both of you, in what way?

_____

_____

_____

_____

_____

_____

How much debt do you have? What kind? How much debt does your significant other have? What kind?

_____

_____

_____

_____

_____

_____

What kind of debt are you willing to incur? Not willing to incur? What kind of debt is your significant other willing to incur? Not willing to incur?

_____

_____

_____

_____

_____

_____

Do you pay your bills on time? If not, why not? If not, how does your significant other feel about this?

_____
_____
_____

Does your significant other pay his or her bills on time? If not, why not? If not, how do you feel about this?

_____
_____
_____

If the two of you were to get married, how do each of you think the banking should be handled (i.e. joint account, separate accounts, separate and joint accounts combined) and why? Will there be any money that the other can't get his or her hands on?

_____
_____
_____
_____
_____
_____

What does budgeting mean to each of you? Does either one of you believe that budgeting is not necessary? How do each of you think the budgeting should be handled and who does each of you think should handle it (one of you or both)?

_____
_____
_____
_____
_____
_____

Would either of you be inclined to keep a stash of money, stocks, bonds, investments, etc., somewhere that the other doesn't know about or that the other knows about but can't get his or her hands on? If so, why?

_____

_____

_____

Does either one of you have beneficiaries? If so, who are they? If you were to get married would you want your beneficiaries to stay the same? Would your significant other want your beneficiaries to stay as is? Would you want the beneficiaries of your significant other to stay as is?

_____

_____

_____

_____

_____

_____

- *Spending habits*

What are your spending habits? What are the spending habits of your significant other?

_____

_____

_____

_____

_____

_____

What is your definition of irresponsible spending? What is your significant other's definition of irresponsible spending?

Does either one of you have a tendency to spend money irresponsibly? If so, explain?

Do you pay bills based on a budget, or do you just pay the bills as they come? If you pay bills based on a budget do you ever stray away from the budget? If so, in what way and how does your significant other feel about this?

Does your significant other pay bills according to a budget, or does he or she just pay the bills as they come? If your significant other pays bills according to a budget, does he or she ever stray from the budget and if so, how do you feel about this?

Do you or does your significant other have any shut off notices? If so, what's about to be shut off and why?

_____

_____

_____

Do you prefer to shop name brand, or are you the type of person who will shop at discount stores, dollar stores, and thrift shops? How does your significant other feel about your spending preferences?

_____

_____

_____

Does your significant other shop name brand, or is he or she the type of person that will shop at discount stores, dollar stores, and thrift shops? How do you feel about his or her spending preferences?

_____

_____

_____

What are the extra things that you spend money on, or would like to spend money on, during the month for your own satisfaction that you feel are essential and are not willing to give up even though you might not necessarily need these things (i.e. clothes, shoes, hair, nails, cable, books, music, video game upkeep, fast food, lawn service, snow removal service, etc)? How often do you spend money on these things during the month? How much money do you spend on these things during the month? How does your significant other feel about you spending money on these extra things?

_____

_____

_____

_____

_____

_____

What are the extra things that your significant other spends money on? How do you feel about him or her spending money on these things? How often is the spending and how much is spent?

_____

_____

_____

_____

_____

What is your definition of a tightwad, a miser, or someone who's frugal when it comes to money? What is your significant other's definition?

_____

_____

_____

Does either one of you consider yourself to be a tightwad, a miser, or frugal, when it comes to money? If so, how does your significant other feel about this? Does either one of you consider the other to be this way?

_____

_____

_____

- **Other finances**

What is your "net worth?" What is the net worth of your significant other (net worth is your assets minus your debts)?

_____

_____

_____

Is either one of you financially contributing to the care of elderly parents, friends, or unemployed relatives? If so, who are you caring for? How much money is being spent and how does your significant other feel about this?

_____

_____

_____

Is either one of you paying child support? If so, how much are you paying? How do these child support payments affect you financially? How does your significant other feel about these payments?

_____

_____

_____

_____

_____

_____

Is either one of you receiving alimony? Is either one of you paying alimony? If so, how does the other of you feel about this?

_____

_____

_____

Does either one of you have parking tickets that haven't been paid? If so, how much are the tickets and why haven't they been paid?

Is either one of you in business? If so, is it a thriving business? If not, will the business deplete the household income? If so, how does your significant other feel about this?

Does either one of you own any stock, real estate, land, or have any investments or trusts? If so, describe.

What does being materialistic mean to you? Do you consider yourself to be materialistic? Do others consider you to be materialistic? If so, how does your significant other feel about this?

What does being materialistic mean to your significant other? Does your significant other consider you to be materialistic? Do you consider your significant other to be materialistic?

Do you pay your income taxes? If not, why not? If so, do you pay them on time? If not, why not? Has the IRS ever audited you? If so, why? What was the outcome?

_____

_____

_____

Does your significant other pay his or her income taxes? If not, why not? If so, does he or she pay them on time? Has the IRS ever audited him or her? If so, why and what was the outcome?

_____

_____

_____

Has your significant other ever cheated on his or her taxes? If so, would he or she want you to cheat on yours?

_____

_____

_____

Has your significant other ever evaded paying taxes? If so, why? Would he or she ever want you to evade paying taxes (especially in cases of self-employment)? If so, why? How do you feel about this?

_____

_____

_____

Do both of you want to live in a house or is one of you satisfied to live in an apartment, a condominium, a flat, etc while the other one wants a house? If one wants a house and the other doesn't, how will the two of you handle this discrepancy?

_____

_____

_____

What is the maximum you are willing to spend on a house and why? What is the maximum monthly mortgage payment you are willing to pay and why?

_____

_____

_____

What is the maximum your significant other is willing to spend on a house and why? What is the maximum monthly mortgage payment your significant other is willing to pay and why?

_____

_____

_____

What is the maximum you are willing to spend on a vehicle? What is the maximum your significant other is willing to spend on a vehicle? Would you prefer to lease a car, buy it new, or buy it used? What is the preference of your significant other? What is the reason for your preference? For your significant other's preference?

_____

_____

_____

_____

_____

If the two of you get married, will each of you have a car? If not, why not?

_____

_____

_____

Does either one of you have any outstanding debts that haven't been paid? If so, explain.

_____

_____

_____

Is either one of you in trouble with the IRS? If so, explain?

_____

_____

_____

Has either one of you been garnisheed or is either one of you being threatened to be garnisheed? If so, please explain.

_____

_____

_____

Does either one of you have a bad credit record? If so, explain?

_____

_____

_____

What debts do each of you owe on a monthly basis?

_____

_____

_____

_____

_____

_____

Has either one of you ever declared bankruptcy or is either one of you on the verge of declaring bankruptcy now? If so, explain.

_____

_____

_____

Work, finances, and money are fought about often in many marriages. So, there is always some compromising that must occur. No two people are alike when it comes to handling cash and assets. Both of you must be willing to compromise within reason. If one of you has a serious spending problem or if the two of you are at total opposite ends of the spectrum as to how money should be budgeted and bills should be paid, then you might want to re-think taking the relationship any further. However, if the two of you have found yourselves to be basically compatible in the area of work, finances, and money, then you may progress to the next chapter.

8.

DIVISION OF LABOR IN AND OUTSIDE OF THE HOME

If the two of you eventually get married, both of you should know beforehand what each of you expects the other to do around the house. The following questions should just about cover it.

- *Household Chores*

Cooking is an everyday thing and a very arduous chore especially if the person doing the cooking does not enjoy cooking. Most families expect three square meals a day and it is difficult to satisfy the taste buds and food preferences of everyone in the family. Each meal can take up to two hours to prepare depending on the size of the family and the food demand of that family. Therefore, the person doing the cooking could easily spend an average of four to six hours a day in the kitchen, which is the equivalent of one part time job.

Who will do the cooking / baking? How often will the cooking be done? Will cooking be a shared responsibility or will it all fall on just one of you? If it will not be a shared responsibility, why won't it?

_____

_____

_____

Who will do the grocery shopping? Will this be a shared responsibility? If not, why not?

_____

_____

_____

Who will do the laundry? Will this be a shared responsibility? If not, why not?

_____

_____

_____

Who will iron the clothes? Will this be a shared responsibility? If not, why not?

_____

_____

_____

Who will pick up the clothes from the cleaners? Will this be a shared responsibility? If not, why not?

_____

_____

_____

Who will make the beds? Will this be a shared responsibility? If not, why not?

_____

_____

_____

Who will do the dusting? Will this be a shared responsibility? If not, why not?

_____

_____

_____

Who will clean the windows? Will this be a shared responsibility? If not, why not?

_____

_____

_____

Who will scrub, sweep, and/or mop the floors? Who will vacuum the rugs? Will this be a shared responsibility? If not, why not?

_____

_____

_____

Who will wash the dishes? Will this be a shared responsibility? If not, why not?

_____

_____

_____

If or when you have small children, who will change the diapers, feed them, give them a bath, take them to school, etc? Will this be a shared responsibility? If not, why not?

_____

_____

_____

When the children become older or if one of you has older children already, who will help the children with their homework? Will this be a shared responsibility? If not, why not?

_____

_____

_____

Who will drive the children around? Will this be a shared responsibility? If not, why not?

_____

_____

_____

Who will mow the lawn, do the gardening, and shovel the snow, rake the leaves, etc.? Will this be a shared responsibility? If not, why not? Will you pay a landscaper to do it?

_____

_____

_____

Who will paint the walls? Will this be a shared responsibility? If not, why not? Will you hire a skilled laborer to do it?

_____

_____

_____

Who will walk the dog, change the kitty litter, and take care of the pets (if you have them)? Will this be a shared responsibility? If not, why not?

_____

_____

_____

Who will do the minor home repairs? Will this be a shared responsibility? If not, why not? Will you hire someone to do home repairs?

_____

_____

_____

If both of you are working, what will each of you expect from the other when both of you get home from work every day?

_____

_____

_____

_____

_____

_____

Not being compatible in this area will have a great bearing on whether or not your marriage will be a happy one or a miserable one. If the two of you cannot basically agree on who will be doing what around the house then it is best that you not take the relationship any further. However, if the two of you are in agreement with the set up of how the division of labor will be in your home, were you to get married, then you may progress to the next chapter.

9.

SEX AND SEX APPEAL

If we are going to live holy as Christians then we have to follow the biblical doctrine which teaches that sex is reserved only for a man and a woman who are married to one another. All other sex outside of a marital union between a man and a woman is biblically immoral. The following passage of scripture, which is found in 1st Corinthians 7, attests to this. It says,

- *Now about the questions you asked in your letter. Yes, it is good to live a celibate life. But because there is so much sexual immorality, each man should have his own wife, and each woman should have her own husband.* (vs.1-2 NLT). This passage of scripture teaches that sex outside of marriage is not permissible.

- *Now to the unmarried and the widows I say: It is good for them to stay unmarried, as I am. But if they cannot control themselves, they should marry, for it is better to marry than to burn with passion* (vs. 8-9 NIV). If it were all right to have sex before marriage then this passage of scripture would teach that those who cannot sexually control themselves are free to go ahead and have sex even if they are not married. But instead, the passage teaches that single people who are having a very difficult time remaining celibate (cannot sexually control themselves) should get married, so that they can have sex and not burn with passion. The only moral way for a Christian to have sex is to so with his or her marriage partner.

Consequently, for Christians who are dating and are living according to biblical standards, there is no sexual testing ground before marriage. Christians are not at liberty to "try it out" with their significant other to see whether or not there is enough sexual compatibility.

However, once a Christian man and woman are married to one another, whether or not both of them are being sexually satisfied in the marriage becomes a major issue. Unfortunately, many Christians do not know what kind of sexual appetite and preferences their significant other has until they marry him or her. Then, if there is any sexual incompatibility, they have found out too late and the marriage suffers greatly from this. For some Christians, the sex is so unsatisfying in their marriage that for them, it has been demoted to the level of just another chore to complete. The passion was gone a long time ago and resentment has set in.

It is important for you to know whether or not you and your significant other are sexually compatible. Since the two of you are Christians, and are therefore not at liberty to have sexual relations before you are married, the only other thing to do in order to determine your compatibility in this area is to ask some questions of one another and talk about it.

Some of you have had previous sexual experiences and may therefore know better what you like or don't like when it comes to sex. Others of you have not had sexual relations. However, those of you in the latter group still have some idea as to which sexual practices you find acceptable and which ones you don't. You probably also have an idea as to what stimulates you sexually. But there may be a few questions that you might not be able to answer since you've never had sex before, and that's okay.

The following questions will help you determine whether or not you and your significant other are sexually compatible. The following questions are hard hitting and some of them might make you feel uncomfortable. But if by asking these questions you discover that you and your partner are not really compatible in the area of sex, you'll be glad you asked about these things regardless as to how uneasy the questions might make you feel now.

As you and your significant other are asking and answering these questions of one another, it would be a good idea to keep in mind (when considering each other's sexual preferences) the last sentence of the verse found in Romans 14:23 which says, *"If you do anything you believe is not right, you are sinning."* (NLT) The operative word is *believe*. So, if something is okay to do, but you don't think it's okay to do, then for you it is a sin and it is not okay to do. And it would be wrong for any brother or sister in the Lord to try to talk you into doing whatever it is that you don't believe is okay to do.

In the Introduction, I indicated that the best way to use this book is for both you and your significant other to have your own individual book and to go through the questions in front of a Christian counselor or pastor. However, the following questions are so very personal that the two of you might not feel comfortable talking in front of someone else. And that's okay, because this book has not only been designed to be an enhancement to the counseling experience, but to also, if necessary, stand alone as a self-help counseling tool. Therefore, the presence of a counselor is preferable, but is not absolutely necessary for determining compatibility, as long as the two of you are totally honest.

A note of caution: most of the questions in this chapter are very explicit and thus may trigger a temptation to engage in sexual relations. Therefore it is strongly suggested (unless, of course, the two of you have chosen to ask these questions of one another in front of a counselor) that you ask these questions of one another over the phone and in phases, instead of all at once.

• *Sexual urges*

How do each of you interpret the following verses of scripture and what do they mean to you?

"The wife's body does not belong to her alone but also to her husband. In the same way, the husband's body does not belong to him alone but also to his wife. Do not deprive each other except by

*mutual consent and for a time, so that you may devote yourselves to prayer..." (*1st Corinthians 7:4-5 NIV).

The operative word in this verse of scripture is "deprive," which means to take away from for a *long period* of time.

_____

_____

_____

How often do you find yourself wanting sex? How often does your significant other find himself or herself wanting sex?

_____

_____

_____

What kind of atmosphere or physical environment puts you in the mood for sex (i.e. lights on, lights off, candles, mirrors, music, silence, etc)? Is it the same or different for your significant other?

_____

_____

_____

What kind of atmosphere or physical environment spoils your mood for sex? Is it the same for your significant other or different? If different, what are the differences?

_____

_____

_____

_____

_____

Is it difficult for you to kiss, hug, and/or cuddle, without progressing to sexual intercourse? If so, how does your significant other feel about this?

_____

_____

_____

Is it difficult for your significant other to kiss, hug, and/or cuddle, without progressing to sexual intercourse? If so, how do you feel about this?

_____

_____

_____

For the man in the relationship, how would you feel about making love to your wife when she's on her period?

_____

_____

_____

For the woman in the relationship, how would you feel about your husband making love to you when you're on your period? How about during the premenstrual time of the month (one to two weeks prior to the onset of your period)?

_____

_____

_____

• *Sexual preferences*

What absolutely turns you off sexually? What absolutely turns your significant other off sexually?

_____

_____

_____

What absolutely turns you on sexually? What absolutely turns your significant other on sexually?

_____

_____

_____

For one reason or another, there are some people who find French kissing repulsive. Are you someone who does? If so, how does your significant other feel about this? Is your significant other someone who does? If so, how do you feel about this?

_____

_____

_____

Would either of you want to participate in oral sex? If not, why not? If so, in what way (giving, receiving, or both)? If so, is this type of sex something that is a "must" for you? For your significant other? Do you think this type of sex between husband and wife is compatible with Christianity? If so, in what way? If not, why not? Does your significant other think this type of sex between husband and wife is compatible with Christianity? If so, in what way? If not, why not? Are there any passages of scripture that would make you or your significant other feel uneasy about engaging in this type of sex? If so, what passages?

_____

_____

_____

Would either of you want to participate in anal sex (sodomy)? If not, why not? If so, is this type of sex something that is a "must" for you? For your significant other? Do you think this type of sex between husband and wife is compatible with Christianity? If so, in what way? If not, why not? Does your significant other think this type of sex between husband and wife is compatible with Christianity? If so, in what way? If not, why not? Are there any passages of scripture that would make you or your significant other feel uneasy about engaging in this type of sex? If so, what passages?

Would either of you want to participate in any form of sadist-masochistic sexual behavior (whips, handcuffs, chains, bondage, etc.)? If not, why not? If so, why? Is this type of behavior during sex something that is a "must" for you? For your significant other? Do you think this type of sexual behavior between husband and wife is compatible with Christianity? If so, in what way? If not, why not? Does your significant other think this type of sexual behavior between husband and wife is compatible with Christianity? If so, in what way? If not, why not? Are there any passages of scripture that would make you or your significant other feel uneasy about engaging in this type of sexual behavior? If so, what passages?

Does either one of you buy pornographic magazines, movies? If so, for what purpose? Has either of you bought pornographic magazine or movies in the past? If so, how long ago? Is this compatible with Christianity?

Would either of you want to use pornographic movies or magazines as a catalyst for sexual arousal? If so, how does your significant other feel about this? Do you think this type of sexual behavior is compatible with Christianity? Are there any passages of scripture that would make you or your significant other feel uneasy about engaging in this type of sexual behavior? If so, what passages?

Would either of you want to videotape the two of you making love to one another once you are married to be later viewed by the two of you only? If not, why not? If so, why? And how does the other one feel about this? Do you think this kind of video taping is compatible with Christianity? Are there any passages of scripture that would make you or your significant other feel uneasy about engaging in this type of sexual behavior? If so, what passages?

_____

_____

_____

Would either of you want to use "sex toys" when making love to your spouse? If not, why not? If so, what kind of sex toys? And how does the other one feel about this? Are there any passages of scripture that would make you or your significant other feel uneasy about engaging in this type of sexual behavior? If so, what passages?

_____

_____

_____

What does the following scripture mean to you and to your significant other?

Marriage should be honored by all, and the marriage bed kept pure, for God will judge the adulterer and all the sexually immoral." (Hebrews 13:4 NIV). The same scripture in the Amplified Bible reads as such: *"Let marriage be held in honor [esteemed worthy, precious, of great price, and especially dear] in all things. And thus let the marriage bed be undefiled [undishonored]; for God will judge and punish the unchaste [all guilty of sexual vice] and adulterous."*

_____

_____

_____

_____

_____

The missionary sexual position (man on top, woman at bottom) is the most widely used sexual position. Are there any other sexual positions that either one of you prefer? If so, what are they? Are there any positions that either one of you would be opposed to? If so, what are they and why the opposition?

_____
_____
_____
_____
_____
_____

Would either of you want to make love in places other than a bedroom (i.e. car, the floor, the tub, the woods, etc)? If not, why not? If so, where? How does the other one feel about this?

_____
_____
_____
_____
_____
_____

Would either one of you consider having sexual intercourse while dressed or partially dressed? If so, how does the other feel about this?

_____
_____
_____

How important is foreplay to you? To your significant other? Would either of you be willing to have sexual intercourse with your spouse without foreplay? If not, why not? If so, how often?

_____
_____

_____

_____

Is sexual spontaneity important to you? To your significant other? If so, in what way?

_____

_____

_____

Is sexual preparation important to you (i.e. what to wear to bed, perfumes-colognes, the feel of the sheets, etc.,)? If not, why not? If so, in what way? Is it important to your significant other? If not, why not? If so, in what way?

_____

_____

_____

_____

Would either of you ever ask the other for a "threesome?" If so, stop right here, close the book, and break off the relationship. This is unacceptable in a Christian marriage.

* *Past sexual experiences*

How do you define "cheating"?

_____

_____

_____

How does your significant other define cheating?

_____

_____

_____

Has your significant other ever "cheated" on you? If so, what is the reason that was given?

_____

_____

_____

Have you ever "cheated" on your significant other? If so, why?

_____

_____

_____

Has your significant other ever cheated on anyone in a past relationship, or cheated on his or her previous spouse, or had an "affair" with someone who was married? If so, expound. Do you trust your significant other to be faithful? If so, expound.

_____

_____

_____

_____

Have you ever "cheated" on anyone in a past relationship, or if you've been married before, did you cheat on your spouse, or have you ever had an affair with someone who was married? If so, expound. Does your significant other trust you to be faithful?

_____

_____

_____

_____

Does either one of you have a history of prostitution? If so, explain.

_____

_____

_____

Has either one of you ever been involved in bestiality (sex with animals)? If so, explain.

_____

_____

_____

Has either one of you ever been the perpetrator or victim of incest? If so, expound.

_____

_____

_____

Has either one of you ever been raped, sexually assaulted, or sexually abused? If so, when did this happen, who was the abuser, and how has this affected your outlook towards the opposite sex? Have you ever received counseling? Do you think you will be able to eventually talk about this with your significant other (if you haven't already)?

_____

_____

_____

_____

_____

_____

• *Sexual difficulties*

Has the man in the relationship ever had any problems with impotence, premature ejaculation, and/or something similar? If so, has he been treated? If not, why not? If so, what was the outcome and does he know whether or not the problem still exists?

Has the woman in the relationship ever had difficulty reaching an orgasm during sex or ever experienced chronic painful intercourse? If so, when and how often? If so, has she ever been treated? If so, what was the outcome and does she know whether or not the problem still exists?

• *Other sexual concerns*

Is the man in the relationship circumcised? If not, how does the woman in the relationship feel about this?

Has the woman in the relationship had a breast augmentation, a breast reduction, or breast reconstruction done? If so, how does the man in the relationship feel about this?

_____

_____

_____

Has either one of you had a mastectomy or partial mastectomy (men can get breast cancer too)? Is either breast prosthetic? If so, how does your significant other feel about this?

_____

_____

_____

Has either one of you had any reconstructive, plastic, or cosmetic surgery of any kind? If so, what kind of surgical or medical procedure was done and how does the other one feel about this?

_____

_____

_____

Do you see the act of having sex as more of a physical fulfillment for you or more of an emotional fulfillment? Can your significant other say the same?

_____

_____

_____

Do you believe in birth control? If not, why not? If so, do you plan to use birth control? If not, why not? If so, what kind of birth control will you be using?

_____

_____

_____

Does your significant other believe in birth control? If not, why not? If so, does he or she plan to use birth control? If not, why not? If so, what kind of birth control will he or she be using?

_____

_____

_____

Do you want your significant other to use birth control? If not, why not? If so, why? What type? Is there any type of birth control that you are absolutely opposed to?

_____

_____

_____

Does your significant other want you to use birth control? If not, why not? If so, why? What type? Is there any type of birth control that your significant other is absolutely opposed to?

_____

_____

_____

• *Sexual Attraction and Sex Appeal*

Is weight a sexual turn off to you? If so, is your significant other overweight in your eyes? If so, can you live with this? Do you expect your significant other to lose weight? Does your significant other see himself or herself as overweight and if so, overweight to a fault? If your significant other is not overweight but should ever become overweight, how will you respond?

_____

_____

_____

_____

_____

_____

Is weight a sexual turn-off to your significant other? If so, are you overweight in his or her eyes? If so, can he or she live with this? Does your significant other expect you to lose the weight? Do you see yourself as overweight and if so, overweight to a fault? If you're not overweight, how will your significant other respond if you should ever become overweight?

_____

_____

_____

_____

_____

_____

If you're the man in the relationship, how do you feel about a woman wearing makeup? Wearing fake nails? Painting her nails? Not painting her nails? Using a perm, coloring, relaxing, weaving, pressing, cutting, teasing, braiding, dread locking, dying her hair, or wearing it in an "Afro"? How does your significant other feel about these things? For you, which of these things add to or take away from the sexual attractiveness of a woman, if any?

_____

_____

_____

If you are the woman in a relationship, how do you feel about balding or bald men? Men with beards? Men with mustaches? Men without them? Men who (some actually do) wear makeup? Men who (some do this too) paint their nails? Men who color, perm, weave, press, cut, braid, dye their hair, wear their hair in an afro, wear their hair in dreadlocks, or let their hair grow long? How does your significant other feel about these things? For you, which of these things add to or take away from the sexual attractiveness of a man, if any?

_____

_____

_____

What kind of attire is sexually appealing to you? To your significant other?

_____

_____

_____

What kind of attire is sexually unappealing to you? To your significant other?

_____

_____

_____

If you're the man in the relationship, are small-breasted ("flat-chest") women, and/or women with sagging breasts, and/or women with stretch marks, and/or women with flat shaped posteriors, and/or women with very thin lips, and/or women with facial wrinkles, and/or women with facial hair, a sexual turn-off to you? If so, does your significant other have either of these physical characteristics? If so, is this something you think you can live with? If not, what is your solution? Would you want her to have something surgically or medically done in order to achieve what you think would be an improvement or are you willing to accept her as she already is?

_____
_____
_____

Is there any physical characteristic about your significant other, that hasn't been covered, that turns you off sexually in which surgery or some kind of medical procedure would be the only solution available in order to achieve what you would consider to be an improvement? If so, what is the characteristic? Would you insist on the surgery?

_____
_____
_____

Is there any physical characteristic about you, that hasn't been covered, that turns your significant other off sexually in which surgery or some kind of medical procedure would be the only solution available in order to achieve what he or she would consider an improvement? If so, what is the characteristic? Would your significant other insist on the surgery?

_____
_____
_____

If you're the woman in the relationship, would a man with a small penis, when erect, be a sexual turn-off to you? If so, what is your definition of "small"? If so, have you asked your significant other about this? If he tells you that he does have a small penis, can you live with this? If you can't, what is your solution?

_____
_____
_____

If you're the man in the relationship, are there any physical characteristics that a woman "must have" in order for you to be sexually turned on? If so, what are they and does your significant other have them? If she doesn't, what is your solution?

_____

_____

_____

If you're the woman in the relationship, are there any physical characteristics that a man "must have" in order for you to be sexually turned on? If so, what are they and does your significant other have them? If he doesn't, what is your solution?

_____

_____

_____

What kind of personality is sexually appealing to you? To your significant other? What kind of personality is a sexual turn-off to you? To your significant other?

_____

_____

_____

• *Other important sexual issues*

Does either one of you have any sexual abnormalities (underdeveloped genitalia, overdeveloped genitalia, ambiguous genitalia, hermaphrodite physicalities, etc)? If so, what are they?

_____

_____

_____

Does either one of you have any physical imperfections or deformities that the other does not know about (i.e. burns, scars, skin diseases, discoloration, moles, warts, tattoos, cellulite, spider veins, keloids, tumors, growths, a prosthesis, pacemaker etc.,)? If so, what are they and how does your significant other feel about this?

_____

_____

_____

Has either one of you had a colostomy? If so, how do the two of you think this will affect your sex life if you get married?

_____

_____

_____

Is either one of you incontinent? If so, how do the two of you think this will affect your sex like if you get married?

_____

_____

_____

Has either one of you ever lived a homosexual life or been involved in a homosexual relationship? If so, is this something that is truly in the past, or are you still tempted in this area?

_____

_____

_____

Does either one of you have homosexual or pedophile fantasies? If so, how often and when?

_____
_____
_____

Has either one of you ever considered yourself to be bisexual? If so, explain. If so, is this truly in the past?

_____
_____
_____

Is either one of you now, or has either one of you ever been, a cross dresser / transvestite? If so, explain.

_____
_____
_____

Is either one of you a transsexual? If so, the relationship must end. This is biblically unacceptable.

_____
_____
_____

Has either of you ever been sexually harassed on the job or anywhere else? If so, what came of it and how did it affect your outlook towards the opposite sex?

_____
_____
_____

Has either one of you ever sexually harassed anyone on the job, or anywhere else? If so, explain.

_____

_____

_____

Has either of you ever been *accused* of sexually harassing someone, sexually abusing someone, or sexually assaulting someone? If so, explain?

_____

_____

_____

Has either one of you ever had sexual temptations towards children? If so, explain. Has either of you ever had sex with someone who was underage? If so, explain. Has either one of you ever sexually abused a child? If so, explain.

_____

_____

_____

Are there any reproductive problems that either of you have that you need to make your significant other aware of (i.e. low sperm count, inability to conceive, irregular periods, hysterectomy, miscarriages, etc)? Has the woman had her "tubes tied"? Has the man had a vasectomy?

_____

_____

_____

Does either one of you *currently* have a venereal disease (i.e. herpes, gonorrhea, chlamydia, genital warts, syphilis, HIV, AIDS, etc)? If so, what disease is it? Are you being treated? If so, what is the prognosis?

_____

_____

_____

Has either one of you *ever had* a venereal disease or ever been treated for a venereal disease? If so, what disease was it? Was the treatment successful?

_____

_____

_____

If the two of you have found out that you are grossly incompatible sexually, then you should absolutely not get married. You should also not get married if you have discovered that your significant other insists on engaging in any sexual activity that is condemned by the Bible or that you *believe* is condemned by the Bible.

As discussed earlier, the desire to have sex is the main reason that the Bible encourages men and women to get married. Sex is the catalyst that drives Christians into marriage (the desire to have sexual relations with someone that they love), seeing that Christians are not having sex (or that they are, at least, not supposed to be having sex) before marriage. Since, for Christians, lack of sexual control is the main reason that is biblically given as to why one should enter into marriage; a good sex life is essential to a happy marriage. Of course, there are other things besides a satisfying sex life that are needed to make a marriage work. But you can be sure that if the sex isn't working, then the marriage isn't working either.

If after answering the questions in this chapter, the two of you believe that if you were to get married, *both of you* would have a satisfying sex life, then you may progress to the next chapter.

10.

DOMESTIC VIOLENCE

Of those who are reported victims of domestic violence, 97% are women. Of those who are reported perpetrators of domestic violence 97% are men (3% are women). Unfortunately, these statistics don't decrease in Christian marriages. Over 50% of the women murdered in the United States each year were murdered by their boyfriend, fiancé, husband, or by a male family member. Of this percentage, roughly 42% of these women were murdered by their husbands. Every 9 seconds a woman becomes the victim of domestic violence. Domestic violence is defined as violence that is perpetrated against someone by someone else who lives in the home (or used to live in the home) with him or her. In general, 70% of all assaults that are perpetrated against women are carried out by the woman's husband, ex-husband, estranged husband, boyfriend, or estranged boyfriend.

A third of the adult population of women have been or will be the victim of domestic violence at least once during their lifetime. A smaller percentage of men will also be victims of domestic violence perpetrated by women. Some of the behavioral signs to look for which profile a man or a woman who might be prone to domestic violence include but are not limited to the following: past history of physical violence towards the opposite sex, controlling behavior, verbal abuse, sexual abuse, unreasonable jealousy, lying, unreasonable expectations, argumentative behavior, an explosive personality, the tendency to minimize or justify the abusive behaviors of themselves or others, attempts to isolate the victim from family, friends, and associates, a history of animal cruelty, and a tendency to push his or her children to achieve beyond their capabilities.

Although much progress has been made in exposing the problem of domestic violence (specifically when it comes to domestic violence against women and the protection of those women) society still has a tendency to "blame the victim" particularly when it comes to women. It will first fault a woman (victimized by domestic violence) for getting involved with an abuser (and for not having had picked up the signs) before it faults a man for the abuse itself. Western society is just now getting to the point where it not only provides services for the victims of domestic violence but the courts are finally beginning to mandate counseling for those who abuse.

The following questions should be asked over the phone because if indeed your significant other has a tendency towards violence, these questions could incite him or her.

* *Physical and verbal abuse*

Has either one of you ever hit, pushed, slapped, bit, punched, thrown something at, cursed at, someone (particularly a member of the opposite sex)? If so, who, how often, what was the result of this behavior?

_____

_____

_____

_____

_____

_____

Has any woman ever accused the man in the relationship of hitting or attacking her, but he denies it?

_____

_____

_____

Has any man ever accused the woman in the relationship of hitting or attacking him, but she denies it?

_____

_____

_____

Has either one of you ever been *accused* of rape, sexual assault, sexual abuse, or sexual harassment by anyone? If so, explain. If not, both of you should check the National Sex Offenders Registry anyway, to be certain of the other.

_____

_____

_____

If your significant other has physically assaulted or cursed at a member of the opposite sex in previous times, how many different people did he or she hit and why?

_____

_____

_____

Have you or has your significant other ever felt a need to restrain yourself from hitting a person of the opposite sex? If so, what led to this point?

_____

_____

_____

Have you or has anyone else ever filed a personal protection order against your significant other? If so, why?

_____

_____

_____

Has your significant other ever filed a personal protection order against someone else? If so, why?

_____

_____

_____

Has either one of you ever filed a personal protection order against the other, drawn a weapon on the other, and/or yelled at, hit, pushed, threatened, cursed, and/or thrown something at the other? If so, dissolve the relationship immediately.

Has anyone ever pressed charges against you or against your significant other? If so, why?

_____

_____

_____

Have you or has your significant other ever called a member of the opposite sex out of his or her name (this is not exclusive to profanity)?

_____

_____

_____

Have you or has your significant other ever drawn a weapon on anyone? If so, why and what was the outcome?

_____

_____

Has anyone ever drawn a weapon on you or on your significant other? If so, expound.

Have you or has your significant other ever carried a concealed weapon? If so, why?

Has either one of you ever killed someone, threatened to kill someone, murdered someone, or seriously considered murdering someone? If so, explain.

• *Behavior that is controlling*

Behavior that is controlling is not always easy to discern. Most people who are controlling don't show how truly controlling they really are until they are married. However, there are definitely those people who are obviously and aggressively controlling right from the start. People who are controlling want things their way all the time and like to tell other people what to do. They also have a very difficult time accepting the opinions of others that differ from theirs. They can be very self-righteous, stubborn, arrogant, and quite demanding. A controlling Christian, if he or she is married, will more often than not want to have control over the ministry that the Lord has given his or her spouse.

Controlling behavior is often times masked as caring behavior. But there are some things to watch for. If you find yourself frequently telling your significant other that he or she is controlling or if you find yourself feeling controlled, even just now and then, this could turn into a big problem once you're married.

Does your significant other often tell you what to wear, what to eat, what to drink, what to say, how to think? If so, in what way?

_____

_____

_____

Do you feel that your significant other sometimes talks to you as if you were a child? If so, in what way?

_____

_____

_____

Does your significant other want a lot of say when it comes to your ministry? Does he or she try to take control of the ministry the Lord has given you? If so, in what way?

_____

_____

_____

_____

_____

Do you feel that your significant other frequently quotes certain scriptures in an effort to try to control you? If so, which scriptures are often quoted?

If you're the woman in the relationship, does your significant other often point to the verses of scripture that talk about women submitting to their husbands? Does he often point to the verses of scripture that talk about men being the head of the house? If so, what does he say about these things? How often does he point to these passages of scripture?

If you're the woman in the relationship, does your significant other believe that being the head of the house means he's always in control, always in charge, what he says goes, etc? If so, what exactly does he say to you about these things?

If you're the woman in the relationship, does your significant other believe that God will speak to a woman's husband about an issue, or about spiritual matters, or about a ministry before he speaks to her?

Is your significant other always telling you what to do? If so, what are some of the things he or she tells you to do all of the time?

_____

_____

_____

Does your significant other allow you to think independently of him or her or must you always agree with what he or she says?

_____

_____

_____

Can you disagree with your significant other without a problem?

_____

_____

_____

Can you disagree with the opinion of your significant other about something in front of others (courteously, of course) without a problem?

_____

_____

_____

Does your significant other become angry or unsettled when you suggest to him or her what to do?

_____

_____

_____

Do you feel that you must be careful what you say, how you look, and how you behave when you are with your significant other? In essence, do you feel as if you're "walking on eggshells" around him or her? If so, in what way?

_____

_____

_____

Would your significant other insist that you vote for the same candidate that he or she votes for? If so, why?

_____

_____

_____

• *Jealousy and possessiveness*

Does your significant other have a jealous streak? If so, in what way?

_____

_____

_____

Is your significant other constantly accusing you of being with someone else and/or of being unfaithful to him or her? If so, who is he or she accusing you of and why the accusations?

_____

_____

_____

Do you feel that your significant other has a suffocating personality (i.e. wants to be around you constantly, wants to know your every move and whereabouts, calls you frequently during the day, and gets upset if you cannot readily be reached by phone)? If so, in what way?

_____

_____

_____

Do you feel that your significant other is possessive (i.e. doesn't want you to be with anyone else or do anything for anyone else, even if it is for your family and friends)? If so, in what way?

_____

_____

_____

Does your significant other try to isolate you from family and friends. If so, how?

_____

_____

_____

• *Anger*

Does your significant other have a bad temper, even if it's just now and then? If so, how does he or she display it? Proverbs 22:24 says, "*do not make friends with a hot-tempered man, do not associate with one easily angered.*" (NIV). Therefore, if either one of you has a bad temper, then the relationship should be dissolved.

_____

_____

_____

Is your significant other argumentative and contentious? If so, what is it that he or she seems to argue about most of the time? Does it feel like it's anything and everything?

_____

_____

_____

Can you disagree with your significant other without him or her becoming unraveled, discombobulated, and/or irritated? If not, why not?

_____

_____

_____

Do the two of you argue a lot when you are with one another? If so, why? What do you argue about?

_____

_____

_____

Do you feel that your significant other has a strong need to always be right about everything and never be wrong about anything? If so, how do you feel about this?

_____

_____

_____

Does it seem as if your significant other always has to "one up" you. If so, how?

_____

_____

_____

Does your significant other frequently make snide remarks? Is your significant other often sarcastic? Condescending? Belittling? If so, in what way?

_____

_____

_____

Does your significant other always have to have the last word? Does he or she have to "win?"

_____

_____

_____

* **Criminal behavior**

Has your significant other ever been arrested? If so for what?

_____

_____

_____

Has your significant other ever been convicted of a felony or misdemeanor? If so, what are the circumstances behind this?

_____

_____

_____

Has your significant other ever been on probation for anything? If so, for what?

Has your significant other ever been to jail or prison? If so, for what? If he (or she) says that he (or she) hasn't but you have doubts, ask a member of his (or her) family or ask for enough information so that you can double check the criminal check sites available on the Internet.

Has your significant other ever involved himself or herself in criminal or illegal activity? If so, has he or she stopped engaging in this activity? If so, what kind of criminal or illegal activity was it?

- *Treatment of the ex-spouse*

If your significant other has been divorced, have you asked to see his or her divorce papers? If you haven't, ask to see them. If he or she refuses to let you see them, ask why not. Marriage licenses and divorce papers are a matter of public record. You can view any of these records in any state at your city, county, or state municipal building. Or, upon request, you can acquire copies of these records from the Department of Vital Statistics. If your significant other will not let you take a look at his or her divorce papers (which is a big red flag...could it be that he or she is not yet divorced?), you should do what it takes to acquire them on your own.

_____

_____

_____

If your significant other has been married before, how did he or she get along with the ex? Ask if it's all right for you to give the ex a call to ask some questions. If your significant other resists, this may be a red flag. Ask your significant other why he or she is resisting.

_____

_____

_____

If you were able to talk to your significant other's ex about some things, what did you learn about him or her?

_____

_____

_____

If your significant other is divorced. Was he or she the one who filed for divorce? If so, why? If not, why did the ex-spouse file?

_____

_____

_____

How many times has your significant other been married and divorced? If more than once, there may be some cause to be concerned, especially if his or her ex-spouses were the ones who filed for divorce. What's the explanation that has been given for these multiple marriages and divorces?

_____

_____

_____

_____

Does your significant other often blame his or her ex for everything that went wrong in the previous marriage or relationship? If so, in what way?

_____

_____

_____

- *Parental relationships*

Has your significant other ever yelled at, hit, or cursed at his or her parents, or any other family member? If so, when and why?

_____

_____

_____

Was your significant other abused, bullied, or picked on as a child? If so, in what way and by whom?

_____

_____

_____

Did your significant other abuse, bully, or pick on others as a child. If so, who was bullied and in what way?

_____

_____

_____

Some people were abused as children and don't realize it, won't acknowledge it, or won't accept it. If your significant other received spankings as a child, how extensive were those spankings? Would you describe those spankings as abusive? Would your significant other describe those spankings as abusive?

What other kinds of punishment did your significant other receive as a child from his or her parents or caretakers when he or she did something against the rules?

Did your significant other grow up in a family environment of domestic violence? If so, ask him or her to tell you about it.

How does your significant other treat his or her parents, sisters, brothers, and family members in general?

Has your significant other, ever (even if only just once), witnessed either of his or her parents hit, yell at, or curse at the other parent? If so, what happened?

Was your significant other ever humiliated, embarrassed, and/or cursed at by either of his or her parents/caretakers? If so, which parent and to what extent?

• *More things to consider*

Has your significant other ever made you the butt of his or her jokes, embarrassed you in front of others, humiliated you in front of others, made fun of you, excessively teased you, mocked you, etc? If so, when and where does this happen? How often does this happen? How do you feel about this when it happens? Does your significant other justify his or her behavior (when and if you complain) by questioning your sense of humor, minimizing what he or she has said or done, accuse you of being too sensitive, telling you you're overreacting)?

Does your significant other have a valid driver's license? If not, why not? If so, ask to see it.

_____

_____

_____

Has your significant other ever used illegal drugs or used drugs illegally? If so, what kind? Has he or she quit? If so, how long ago. If not, why not? Has he or she ever sold drugs?

_____

_____

_____

How long does it take your significant other to return a phone call? If longer than 24 hours, why?

_____

_____

_____

Does your significant other keep promises? If not, what promises haven't been kept and why haven't they been kept?

_____

_____

_____

Has your significant other ever stood you up? If so, why and how many times?

_____

_____

_____

If you're the woman in the relationship, does your significant other have a reputation of being a womanizer (defined as a man who has relationships with many women either simultaneously or one right after the other)? If so, what is his explanation for having this type of reputation?

_____

_____

_____

If you're the man in the relationship, does your significant other have a reputation for being a man chaser? If so, what is her explanation for having this type of reputation?

_____

_____

_____

Does your significant other often blame you for things that go wrong between the two you? If so, what are some of the things you're blamed for?

_____

_____

_____

Has your significant other ever stalked anyone either physically, by e-mail, by phone, or by some other means? If so, what is his or her explanation for this?

_____

_____

_____

How do other people see your significant other? Does he or she have a bad reputation? If so, what kind?

_____

_____

_____

Has anybody tried to "warn" you about your significant other? If so, what have they said?

_____

_____

_____

Does your significant other often criticize you? If so, what does he or she criticize you about and why? Does he or she bully you or others? If so, in what way and why?

_____

_____

_____

If your significant other *is abusive in any way*, you should not marry him or her. Remember, whatever negative behavior there is that is apparent during the dating stage will increase a hundred-fold in a marriage. And if your significant other has answered all of these questions perfectly but you still have a hunch that he or she is keeping some important details from you, then it wouldn't hurt to have a background check done. This may sound extreme but it really is better to be safe than sorry. However, if (and only if) the two of you were able to get through these questions without either one of you feeling that the other is prone to being abusive and/or violent, then you may progress to the next chapter.

11.

WHAT IF?

There are things that happen in life that can test the love a person has for you and that you have for another. It is good to know how far someone's love really goes before marrying him or her. In asking the following questions of one another you will be better able to measure whether or not both of you love each other to the same degree. These questions should be asked by imagining that the two of you are already married.

What would happen if one of you were somehow sexually incapacitated for a long period of time? Would the other stay? Does the other think that he or she might be tempted towards adultery because of this?

_____

_____

_____

What would happen if one of you were to become physically incapacitated for a long period of time or for life? Would the other stay? Does the other think that he or she might be tempted towards adultery because of this?

_____

_____

_____

What would happen if one of you had to have a body part amputated? Would the other stay? Does the other think that he or she might be tempted towards adultery because of this?

_____

_____

_____

What would happen if one of you were to become facially disfigured? Would the other stay? Does the other think that he or she might be tempted towards adultery because of this?

_____

_____

_____

What would happen if one of you felt you had to suddenly take care of some children in the family (the parents of the children die in a car crash, a family member is on drugs and cannot properly care for his or her children, etc)?

_____

_____

_____

What would happen if the two of you had a child that was born less than perfect (i.e. profound retardation, profound physical ailment, profound handicap, profound deformity, profound mental incapacity)?

_____

_____

_____

How would both of you feel and what would happen if you knew your child was going to be less than perfect before he or she was born?

_____

_____

_____

What would happen if the two of you decided to have children but discovered that you were unable to have children together? Would either or you consider any of the following: adoption, in vitro fertilization, a surrogate carrier, or a sperm bank? If so, do both of you think these considerations are compatible with Christianity?

_____

_____

_____

If one of your parents became ill and were not able to care for his or herself, how would your significant other feel about you moving your Mom or Dad into the house? Would your significant other prefer that your parent be placed into a nursing home? How would you feel about moving in one or both of your significant other's parents to take care of him or her? If this were to happen, who would be the main caretaker and why?

_____

_____

_____

_____

_____

What would happen if one of you were to suffer a "nervous breakdown" which progressed into an on-going severe mental illness, such as schizophrenia, manic-depression, etc., requiring hospitalization and psychotropic medication? Would the other one stay? Would the other one be prone to commit adultery?

_____

_____

_____

Although these are just "what ifs" there is a very real possibility that one of these things could happen. Granted, it is very difficult for someone to really say what they'd do in many of the situations described in this chapter and a person might sincerely feel that he or she could handle a thing until that thing comes about. However, if both of you feel comfortable with the answers that you've given regarding these things, then you may progress to the next chapter.

12.

PERSONALITY

No two people have personalities that are one hundred percent compatible. However, there are some personality differences that when combined together have the potential to complicate a relationship more so than the combination of other personality differences. And there are other personalities that can stand alone as a barrier to the success of a relationship. In this chapter we will look at some personality combinations and some stand-alone personalities that can cause damage to a promising relationship.

- ***Extrovert vs. Introvert***

An extrovert is a gregarious person who rarely hesitates to express his or her opinions, is assertive, sociable, adventurous, and eager to be involved in activities. An introvert, on the other hand, prefers time alone, may be shy, and is less expressive of himself or herself. Introverts often like to stay at home as opposed to going out and they are not prone to feeling lonely.

If these two personalities are dating one another then both parties must be willing to do some compromising. The extrovert should be careful not to be critical of the fact that the introvert is not as outgoing and assertive as the extrovert is. And the introvert must be willing to accept the fact that the extrovert likes being around people and going places. If the extrovert is not careful, he or she will find himself or herself being an imposition upon the introvert. For example, an extrovert is more likely to invite people over to the house just to be sociable or friendly, but this may be very imposing for an introvert whose refuge is his or her home.

Does either one of you believe that one of you is an extrovert while the other is an introvert? If so, how are the two of you handling this difference in personality?

_____

_____

_____

- *Talkative vs. Non-Talkative*

Some people are very talkative while other people don't say much unless they have to. Non-talkative people are often times misunderstood. It is not that they're being anti-social it's just that whatever is being discussed must be about something that is substantially interesting or important to them for them to be inspired to take part in the conversation.

On the other hand talkative people like to talk and are willing to talk about many things. Talkative people are also more likely to enjoy talking on the phone as opposed to non-talkative people.

Very talkative people will talk about almost anything. Extremely talkative people must be careful not to monopolize a conversation. If extremely talkative people are not careful they will be the only ones talking during a conversation. Very talkative people can talk for hours on one subject.

It is very distressing for someone who likes to talk to try to talk to someone who's not very talkative. The non-talkative person is often times more of a "let's get to the point" type of person and has little need to belabor an issue while the talkative person may have a tendency or a need to cover an issue thoroughly in order to find closure or a resolution.

If two people are dating and are on the extreme ends of these opposite personalities, then the relationship could suffer. Non-talkative people can be very guarded about disclosing their feelings because they often associate the disclosure with being vulnerable. However, talkative people often talk about how they are feeling about things. In a marriage, the talkative person may eventually become resentful of the fact that his or her partner doesn't talk much, and the less talkative person may feel overwhelmed by his or her partner's need to talk.

Does either one of you believe that one of you is quite a bit more talkative than the other? If so, how are the two of you handling this difference?

_____

_____

_____

- ***Spontaneous personality vs. a planner***

Some people are very spontaneous when it comes to doing things. They don't feel a strong need to plan for special events and are very comfortable in doing things on the spur of the moment. On the other hand there are others who are completely uncomfortable with spontaneity and feel a need to methodically plan each move they make. In a relationship, these two personalities will clash unless both partners commit to giving a little to get a little; in other words, compromising. The spontaneous person must be willing to embrace a plan now and then, and the planner must be willing to bend a bit and be spontaneous at times.

Does either one of you believe that one of you is spontaneous while the other is a planner? If so, how are the two of you handling this difference?

_____

_____

_____

- *Pessimist vs. Optimist*

There are those who are more likely to see the glass as half empty as opposed to half full, when looking at a situation. They see the negative side of things before they see the positive and they often times act on those negative views. People who have this tendency are pessimists. They have an inclination to expect the worse.

On the other hand there are those who are more likely to see the glass as half full rather than half empty. They see the positive side of things before they see the negative and they therefore act on their positive perspective. People who have a tendency to see the bright side of things before looking at the dark side are optimists. They have an inclination to hope for the best.

If these two personalities get together there is a good chance that they could help balance one another if each is open to seeing the other side of things. Problems usually arise with this kind of personality combination when the optimist is not as concerned about something that the pessimist sees as a concern.

Do you consider yourself to be an optimist or a pessimist? How does your significant other see you?

_____
_____
_____

Do you consider your significant other to be an optimist or a pessimist? How does your significant other see himself or herself?

_____
_____
_____

If one of you is a pessimist while the other is an optimist, how do you plan to deal with this kind of personality difference between the two of you?

_____

_____

_____

• *Selfish vs. Generous*

A generous person has more regard for others than he does for himself and has a tendency to give liberally to others. On the other hand, selfish people are those who provide for themselves without regard for others. A selfish person is basically only concerned about his or her own needs or activities, often times at the expense of others. The Bible specifically instructs us as Christians not to be selfish. This instruction is found in Philippians 2:3-4. It reads, *"Do not be selfish; don't live to make a good impression on others. Be humble, thinking of others as better than yourself. Don't think only about your own affairs, but be interested in others, too, and what they are doing."* (NLT)

If a selfish person and a generous person are dating one another, there are bound to be problems. No doubt the selfish person will often be irritated by the generosity of his or her counterpart. And the generous person will often be dismayed by the selfishness of his or her partner. Since the Bible tells us not to be selfish, then being so is more than just a personality flaw, it is a sin and such a flaw would therefore be a great hindrance to a marriage. The selfish spouse must therefore be willing to change.

Do you consider your significant other to be a selfish person? If so, in what way? Is he or she trying to change for the better? If not, how do you plan on handling this if the two of you get married?

Do you consider your significant other to be a generous person? If so, in what way? Do you think that your significant other is overly generous? If so, in what way and how do you plan on handling this if the two of you get married?

Does your significant other consider you to be a selfish person? If so, in what way? How does he or she plan on handling this?

Does your significant other consider you to be a generous person? If so, in what way? Does your significant other think that you are overly generous? If so, in what way and how does he or she plan on handling this if the two of you get married?

---

* *The vindictive personality*

As Christians we are commanded to forgive others as Christ forgave us. Christ forgave our sins by offering himself as a perfect living sacrifice on the cross. Through the shedding of his blood and belief in his Deity, our sins are forgiven and we have salvation. It is often times not an easy thing to forgive someone but if we want God to continue to forgive us then we should practice forgiving others. If we are having a difficult time forgiving someone, then we should ask God to help us forgive that person.

If a person is still holding a grudge, is still bitter, or is still stewing over being mistreated by someone, then chances are, he or she has not forgiven the person who caused the distress. Forgiveness means letting things go, not holding grudges, and not being bitter. However, you can forgive someone and still keep your distance. Losing trust in someone doesn't mean that you haven't forgiven that person.

For example, if your neighbor breaks into your house while you are out of town, then even though you might forgive him, you may never trust him. You'd probably make sure to lock the door every time you left the house and he'd probably be the last person you'd ask to watch the house while you were away. This does not mean you haven't forgiven him. Instead, this means you've lost trust in him and are leery about inadvertently giving him another opportunity to steal something else from you. If you have forgiven him, then this means that you've let the incident go, you're not holding a grudge, you're not stewing over the mistreatment, and you're not bitter. However, you don't have prove you've forgiven him by letting him housesit. You can forgive him from a distance. Forgiving someone does not mean that you have to leave yourself open to be re-abused.

There are those people who are very forgiving. Once an issue is resolved they let it go completely. Some people are even able to genuinely forgive an offending person without ever receiving an apology from the offender.

On the other hand there are those who hold grudges for a very long time. They are easily hurt, and they have a very difficult time forgiving people. Granted there are some offenses that are not easy to forgive. But as Christians, we are to forgive people anyway, no matter what they've done. A person who is at the extreme end of a non-forgiving personality is a person who will hold a grudge for the slightest infraction and is a person who can be vindictive.

Vindictive people like to "get back" at people in some way. Often times, vindictive people express their vindictiveness in passive-aggressive ways (indirect aggression). Vindictive people seek revenge. But the Bible tells us that vengeance belongs to the Lord (not to people) as confirmed in Romans 12:19 which reads, *"Do not take revenge, my friends, but leave room for God's wrath, for it is written: 'It is mine to avenge; I will repay says the Lord.'"* (NIV). It is therefore wrong for people to seek revenge.

Living with a revengeful and vindictive person can be a very difficult thing indeed because eventually that person will become vindictive towards you. For this reason, it is good to be able to determine whether or not your significant other has a vindictive personality. Vindictiveness can show itself in small ways. Don't shrug off the evidence. If you think your significant other might be vindictive, chances are that you're right. Once you marry this person this vindictive personality will be magnified.

Define what vindictiveness means to you and means to your significant other. Does either one of you consider yourself or the other to be a vindictive person? If so, how do the two of you plan on handling this personality problem?

_____

_____

_____

_____

_____

_____

• *The competitive personality*

Most people think it is good to have a competitive personality. However, many people with competitive personalities have a tendency to try to "one up" everyone. They don't want anyone to "outshine" them, especially those close to them and particularly those with whom they may be romantically involved.

It is therefore actually better for a competitive person to be in a relationship with someone who is non-competitive. Otherwise, if both the man and the woman have competitive personalities, chances are they will eventually begin competing against one another. But even if one partner is competitive and the other partner is not, the partner who is competitive has to make certain that he or she doesn't perceive everything in the relationship as some kind of boxing match. People who are extremely competitive have been known to undermine, sabotage, and/or minimize the success or potential success of another especially if they have not made the same or similar strides in their own lives. This type of behavior can have a devastating effect upon a marriage especially where ministry is involved.

If a Christian is heavily involved in a ministry that he or she feels the Lord has called him or her to, then that person will not take kindly to someone who is trying to subvert that ministry in any way. However, in Christian relationships, competitiveness, when it comes to ministry and gifts of the Spirit, is unfortunately where much of the problems between couples lie.

Are you or your significant other competitive? If so, in what way? How does the non-competitive partner feel about the competitiveness of the other? Does either one of you think that the competitiveness might get in the way of the relationship? If so, how do the two of you plan to resolve this issue?

• *Those who take things personally*

There are many people who are very easily insulted. It doesn't take much to hurt their feelings, and it doesn't take much for them to believe that others are questioning their judgement, integrity, character, and the like. In a nutshell, they basically take things the wrong way...often. This means that those involved with people who take things personally find themselves constantly being very careful what they say around them and how they say it. This can be very taxing. It's not easy to "walk a tightrope" all the time.

On the other hand, there are those who are not easily rattled even when they have actually been insulted. They shrug things off easily and rarely take things personally. Usually when they do take things personally, what occurred or was said, was just that...personal.

Do people tell you that you take things personally all the time or that you take things the wrong way? Does your significant other think that you take things personally? Do you think that your significant other takes things personally? If one or both of you have a tendency to frequently take things personally, how will the two of you handle this personality problem?

_____

_____

_____

• *Moodiness*

There are those who maintain the same temperament most of the time. They have the same attitude, character, manners, and so forth on a consistent basis. Then there are those who are subject to changing moods and are often times in a bad mood for what might appear to be no particular reason at all. These are the people who frequently "wake up on the wrong side of the bed" and because of this are often labeled as "moody."

Moody people can't seem to keep their bad moods to themselves. If they are in a bad mood then they make sure that everyone in the house either knows they are in a bad mood or are somehow affected by their bad mood. They set the atmosphere and tone of the house. If they're in a good mood then the social atmosphere in the house is good. However, if they're in a bad mood then the social atmosphere in the house is bad. Those who live with these people often times find themselves being very careful as to what they say or do when the moody person is having a bad day.

With this said, living with a moody person may not be easy, can be discouraging, and is just downright aggravating at times. So, if you see your significant other as moody, then you might want to consider whether or not this is something that you can deal with on a regular basis.

Do you consider yourself moody? If so, what triggers your bad moods? Anything in particular? How do you behave when you're in a bad mood? Does your significant other see you as moody?

Do you see your significant other as moody? If so, how does he or she behave when in a bad mood? What do you think triggers his or her bad moods?

If one of you (or both of you for that matter) is moody, how do the two of you plan on dealing with this type of personality in the relationship?

• *Other personality traits that should be considered*

Do you see your significant other as self-centered or self-absorbed? If so, in what way? Does your significant other see you as self-centered or self-absorbed? If so, in what way?

_____

_____

_____

Do you see your significant other as arrogant? If so, in what way. Does your significant other see you as arrogant? If so, in what way?

_____

_____

_____

Most people want their partners to have some kind of sense of humor. However, we must be mindful that there are those that tend to set the standard for what's funny by what they themselves think is funny. They decide whether or not people have a sense of humor based on whether or not people laugh at what they laugh at. Two people can have a sense of humor but not necessarily find the same things to be funny.

Do you have a sense of humor? Is it important to your significant other for you to have a sense of humor? Does your significant other have a sense of humor? Is it important to you for him or her to have a sense of humor? Do the two of you think the same things are funny? If one of you has very little of a sense of humor, how does the other feel about this?

_____

_____

_____

Do you feel that your significant other is egotistical? If so, how so? How do you think this egotistical behavior will eventually affect the relationship?

_____

_____

_____

Do you feel that your significant other is flirtatious with members of the opposite sex besides you? If so, how do you feel about this and how do you think this will eventually affect your relationship?

_____

_____

_____

No two people have personalities that go perfectly together but some personalities just don't mesh together at all and combining them is a recipe for disaster. So, if either of you have the type of personality that constantly unnerves the other, then it is questionable whether or not a marriage would survive such stress. However, if you honestly feel that your personalities are compatible then you may progress to the next chapter.

13.

OTHER IMPORTANT QUESTIONS

The following questions are a just few more important ones that need to be asked that really don't fit under any of the other compatibility areas that have already been presented.

- *Identity*

Does your significant other use an alias? If so, why? Is he or she who they say they are? Have you seen identification that proves that your significant other is who he or she says he or she is?

_____

_____

_____

Do you or does your significant other have a middle name? A nickname? If so, what is it?

_____

_____

_____

How do you define yourself? How does your significant other define him or herself?

_____

_____

_____

_____

_____

_____

- **Background information**

When and where were you born? When and where was your significant other born? Where were you raised? Where was your significant other raised?

_____

_____

_____

Who raised you? Who raised your significant other?

_____

_____

_____

What kind of education do you have? What kind of education does your significant other have? If one of you has significantly more education than the other, how will this affect your relationship?

_____

_____

_____

_____

What schools did you attend and where are/were these schools located? What schools did your significant other attend and where are/were these schools located?

_____

_____

_____

_____

_____

_____

What kind of experiences did you have growing up that made an impression on you?

_____

_____

_____

_____

_____

_____

What kind of experiences did your significant other have growing up that made an impression on him or her?

_____

_____

_____

_____

_____

_____

• *Additional concerns*

Where do you currently live? Where does your significant other live? If the two of you were to get married, would one of you move in with the other, or would the two of you start anew and move into a new property?

_____

_____

_____

If one of you would move in with the other (if you get married), who would move in with who and why?

_____

_____

_____

Do you put the happiness of your significant other before your own happiness? If so, why? If not, why not?

_____

_____

_____

Does your significant other put your happiness before his or her own happiness? If so, why? If not, why not?

_____

_____

_____

What are your political and social beliefs? Does your significant other share those same beliefs? If not, how do you think this disparity will affect your relationship if the two of you were to marry one another?

_____

_____

_____

_____

_____

What are your ambitions (career, school, travel, business, investments, homes, etc)? What are the ambitions of your significant other? Are your ambitions compatible with the ambitions of your significant other?

_____

_____

_____

Has either one of you ever been investigated by the FBI, CIA, IRS, any other part of the government, any part of the State, children's protective services, adult protective services, the prosecutor's office, the police, etc? If so, explain.

_____

_____

_____

_____

_____

_____

Has either one of you ever thought about committing suicide or ever tried to commit suicide? If so, explain. If so, do you still have suicidal thoughts now? If so, how often? Are you being treated now? Have you ever been treated?

_____

_____

_____

If the two of you decide to get married, would both of you want a wedding? If so, how extravagant? Would both of you want a reception? How much would you want to spend on a wedding? How much would your significant other want to spend on a wedding?

_____
_____
_____

Is there a substantial age difference between the two of you? If so, how do you think this age difference would affect a marriage?

_____
_____
_____

Does either one of you keep a gun in the house? If so, why? What kind of gun is it? If so, is the other of you comfortable with a gun in the house? If so, to whom is the gun registered? If it is not registered, why not?

_____
_____
_____

Has either of you given house keys to someone who doesn't live in your home (sister, mother, brother, friend, etc)? If so, is this person able to walk into your home at will? If so, will you want this person to have keys to your marital home? If so, how does your significant other feel about this?

_____
_____
_____

If your significant other wanted to move out of town or out of the country to advance his or her career, or just for the adventure of it, would you be willing to move? How would you feel about this?

_____

_____

_____

If your significant other wanted to move out of town or out of the country to advance his or her ministry, because he or she felt led of the Lord to do so, how would you feel about this? Would you be willing to move?

_____

_____

_____

Is either one of you contemplating getting cosmetic surgery of any kind? If so, what kind and why?

_____

_____

_____

If the relationship you are in is an interracial one, how do your in-laws to-be feel about interracial marriages? Are any of his or her close family members people you would define as racists? If so, how might this affect the two of you if you were to get married? If you were to have children, how might this affect them?

_____

_____

_____

Does your significant other encourage you in the things you are doing or would like to do? If so, in what way? If not, why not?

_____

_____

_____

Do you encourage your significant other in the things that he or she is doing or would like to do? If so, in what way? If not, why not?

_____

_____

_____

Can you talk to your significant other about things that bother you and about things that go wrong in your day? Does your significant other talk to you about these things?

_____

_____

_____

Is your significant other there for you when you are sick, distressed, under the weather, discouraged, having problems? Or do you find yourself going to someone else for comfort when things aren't going well with you?

_____

_____

_____

Is there anything about your significant other that you find embarrassing? If so, what is it? Is there anything that he or she finds embarrassing about you? If so, what is it?

_____

_____

_____

Who are your heroes (people that you hold in high regard whether dead or alive) and why? Who are the heroes of your significant other and why?

_____
_____
_____
_____
_____
_____

Do you enjoy your significant other's conversation? If not, why not? If so, in what way?

_____
_____
_____

Does your significant other enjoy your conversation? If not, why not? If so, in what way?

_____
_____
_____

Does your significant other really listen to the things you have to say? If not, how does this make you feel and how do you think this would affect the two of you as marriage partners?

_____
_____
_____

Do you or does your significant other have any idiosyncrasies? If so, what are they, and how do you think these idiosyncrasies will affect a marital relationship?

If the two of you were to get married, will both of you always be willing to tell the other of your whereabouts and how you can be reached when away from home? If not, why not?

Does your significant other value your opinions and trust your advice? If not, why not? Do you value the opinion of your significant other and trust his or her advice? If not, why not?

What are four values (i.e. children, family, religion, morality, power, control, health, status, integrity, honesty, spirituality, friends, perfection, money, looks, career, etc) that are most important to you? What are four values that are most important to your significant other? How do you feel about the values of your significant other? How does your significant other feel about your values?

Can the two of you be together without having a conversation and still feel comfortable with one another? If not, why not?

_____
_____
_____

Have you told your significant other that you love him or her? If not, why not? Has your significant other told you that that he or she loves you? If not, why not?

_____
_____
_____

Is there anything about your significant other that you would like to see change? If so, what is it and why?

_____
_____
_____

Is there anything about you that your significant other would like to see change? If so, what is it and why?

_____
_____
_____

Do the two of you agree as to whether or not the woman in the relationship will change her last name, hyphenate her last name, or keep her maiden name, if the two of you get married? If you don't agree, why don't you? What's the solution?

_____
_____
_____

What things to do you absolutely expect out of a marriage and from a marriage partner? What are the things would you absolutely would not tolerate in a marriage?

_____
_____
_____
_____
_____
_____
_____
_____

What things does your significant other absolutely expect out of a marriage and from a marriage partner? What are the things that he or she would absolutely not tolerate in a marriage?

_____
_____
_____
_____
_____
_____
_____
_____

PARTING WORDS

Well that's it! If the two of you have made it this far, it looks like you have the potential of having a great life together if you decide to get married. Of course, there are no guarantees.

To try to think of every question that might be of concern when it comes to the issue of compatibility is nearly impossible. So, there may have been some questions that you thought to ask about which were not presented. Therefore, I've provided some blank lined pages for you in the next "chapter" so that you and your significant other can include questions (and the answers to those questions) that you've thought of that are a concern to you that I may have missed. This is the part where you can write your own chapter!

Hopefully you have found that you and your significant other are compatible enough to take your relationship to the next level. If so, congratulations on your upcoming engagement! But if you have discovered that you are not compatible and that it would be best not to become engaged, then congratulations to you too! You have just diverted a potential catastrophe in your life. It is better to know these things now and dissolve the relationship, than to get married and find out when it is too late. So, if the two of you are not compatible, don't despair. Instead, count your blessings, praise God, and move on.

14.

WRITE YOUR OWN CHAPTER

_____

_____

_____

_____

_____

_____

_____

_____

_____

_____

_____

_____

_____

_____

_____

_____

_____

_____

_____

_____

_____

_____

_____

For Christians who are Seriously Dating or Would Like to Be

For Christians who are Seriously Dating or Would Like to Be